SMART KIDS,
STUPID CHOICES

SMART KIDS, STUPID CHOICES

Dr. Kevin Leman

A DELL TRADE PAPERBACK

A DELL TRADE PAPERBACK
Published by
Dell Publishing
a division of
Bantam Doubleday Dell Publishing Group, Inc.
666 Fifth Avenue
New York, New York 10103

Scripture taken from *The Living Bible,* Copyright © 1971 by
Tyndale House Publishers, Wheaton, Illinois. Used by permission.

Also quoted is *KJV*—Authorized King James Version

ISBN: 0-440-50442-2

Reprinted by arrangement with Regal Books
Printed in the United States of America
Published simultaneously in Canada

March 1992

10 9 8 7 6 5 4 3 2 1

BVG

This book is affectionately dedicated to my dad and mom, John and May Leman, who persistently encouraged me throughout my difficult adolescent years. More importantly, they had the courage to tell me what was right and wrong, and the wisdom to allow me to make the choice.

Thank you to Richard Kuykendall for his invaluable assistance in the research for this book.

Thank you to the many people whose encouragement, support and tireless contributions to the manuscript made this book possible.

And thank *you* for buying this book. Without people like you there wouldn't be any successful books or authors.

Contents

Introduction:
Adolescence Isn't Terminal

I just finished typing those words when the phone rang. It was another harried mother of adolescents, ready to pull her hair out, or worse—another woman who needed to hear the comforting thought that adolescence isn't really terminal, and it won't last forever. It just feels that way sometimes.

The phone call interrupted me, but it was a welcome interruption because it reminded me of the reality of the daily battle undergone by parents of teens and preteens everywhere. And it reminded me of the importance and urgency of this book.

In this particular case, the mother had just refereed yet another battle between her teenage son and daughter. The daughter had won, as she usually did, because she was capable of whining the loudest and holding out the longest. The boy had finally said, "Oh, let her have it her way," but as soon as she had left the room, he had begun to talk about how much he hated her and how he wished she'd just drop dead.

When Mom had tried to get him to stop talking that way,

he had insisted it was true. "And if I had a gun, I'd probably just shoot her."

When talking to him failed to produce anything but further belligerence, Mom had tried to talk to the daughter about being nicer to her brother, but the girl's response was something along the lines of, "I don't care about him anyway. You should hear how he talks about *you* when your back is turned. Besides that, I know you've always liked him best. But *Dad* likes *me* best."

Well, that was only the beginning, and I may have missed a word or two, but I think I got most of it.

Did that sound familiar? If you're the parent of an adolescent, I'm sure at least *some* of it sounded very familiar.

But cheer up . . . because there is a way through the maddening, gray-hair-giving jungle that is adolescence, and it's the purpose of this book to help you find it.

This book is primarily an updated and expanded version of a book I wrote several years ago. Most of what I wrote then was based on two things: (1) head knowledge; (2) my dealings with the thousands of families I had counseled as a practicing psychologist.

I had three children of my own at the time—now I have four—but none of them had yet reached the dreaded age known as adolescence. Now, as I update this, one of my girls is in college and another is a senior in high school. My son is in junior high school and the youngest girl is five years old. I have been through darkest adolescence, and although it hasn't been an unbroken string of sunny skies and days at the beach, I can say that I have "road-tested" all of the principles contained within the pages of this book, and have found that they *do* work, and very well.

You can survive your children's adolescence in one piece, and so can they. You can also remain "in control" as your kids pass through this most difficult period of their lives, and you can come out the other side with your relationships intact.

The adolescent years are most difficult for everyone, and what makes them doubly difficult is that all of the pressures of those years squeeze in on teenagers when they are the most vulnerable, during the time when they are quite capable of making mistakes that can leave permanent scars on their lives.

For example, drugs are available everywhere, from the back alleys of Los Angeles and New York to the rural farm roads of Nebraska and Kansas—and the "Just Say No" campaign has not been enough to prevent the breaking of millions of hearts—of parents and kids alike. Teenage experimentation with drugs can leave scars that last forever.

Today, like never before, kids as young as 12 and 13 years old are being pressured to become sexually active. As one young daughter of hardworking middle-class parents told me, "Nobody wants to be a virgin anymore. Only the nerds are virgins." And yet teenage sex leaves behind its legacy of lasting pain in the form of guilt and psychological scars, unwanted pregnancies, abortions, venereal disease, and now even AIDS. The reaction of some sociologists is to say that we can't stop kids from experimenting with sex, so we'd better give them condoms—even though there have been many studies which show that even the best condoms are far from 100 percent effective when it comes to preventing pregnancy or stopping the spread of disease.

As far as I'm concerned, passing out condoms to teens is like issuing them squirt guns to fight a forest fire. Why rely upon devices that are far from 100 percent effective to combat a disease that is always 100 percent fatal? The answer is in teaching our teenagers that sex is most definitely not a play toy.

Another problem facing our teenagers today is the increasing emphasis on violence and sexuality in the media. It's true that even many PG-rated movies are splattered with profanity, nudity, and sadistic violence. By the time he's an adult, the average American child has witnessed an estimated 20,000 murders on television and in the movies—and then we wonder why we're raising so many teenagers who are uncaring, insensitive, and who find it so easy to laugh at the pain of others.

Don't blame the teenagers. They're merely responding to the stimulation of their environment.

And that brings me to another problem that is an increasing worry for parents of teenagers and preteens in urban areas, and that is the fact that gang violence is escalating on an almost daily basis. In the Los Angeles area, it's rare that you can pick up a daily newspaper without reading an account of a drive-by shooting that left another 14- or 15-year-old boy dead or wounded.

Yes, these are most difficult times for adolescents and their parents.

Now you might think that the problem of adolescence has been around since the beginning of time, but the truth is that adolescence is a phenomenon that did not appear until the last century. In fact, the term "adolescent" was unknown until the Industrial Revolution created societies where the age of economic independence and marriage is delayed past puberty.[1]

In other words, adolescence is a creation of culture, and that's the rub. Because our present culture forces children to go through the long period of dependency called adolescence, we have set them on a collision course with our own parental authority.

It is no wonder that parents struggle with getting through to teenagers to help them make smart decisions, when those same teenagers are not always interested in advice from their parents. Teenagers are well-known for loudly protesting that they are smart enough already. Furthermore, they tend to believe that they are indestructible—or at least way beyond the point of needing any help from someone who is as ancient and as outdated as a parent. Almost every week as I counsel I hear it from the young people themselves:

"Why bother talking to my parents? They're from another planet. It's hopeless."

"Ask my dad for advice? You must be kidding! He doesn't have a clue as to how I feel."

"Look, I'm not a kid anymore. I can handle it myself."

Unfortunately, a great number of teenagers don't handle "it" all that well, no matter what "it" may be.

I've heard this or similar statements from dozens of parents: "I can't understand it. We've put just about all of our time, blood, sweat, and tears into raising our kids, and now who do they listen to? Their friends. Or some rock star who should be locked up!"

YOUR ACTIONS CAN OUTSHOUT THE PEER GROUP

I've had the privilege of knowing some excellent parents, Moms and Dads who did just about everything right. But I have yet to know any parents who were able to completely escape the power of the peer group. Moms and dads of teenagers everywhere know that their children pay much more attention to the ideas and opinions of their schoolmates and friends than they do to what they hear at home. But there is an encouraging note in all of this, and that is that while teenagers seem to ignore what their parents *say* they carefully observe what their parents *do*. The wise parent, then, is the one who opens his life, and not just his mouth, in order to communicate with his teenager.

Unfortunately, many parents don't understand this, and they attempt to communicate with their children from some lofty mountain peak. It won't work.

For example, I remember the case of a mother who came to me for counseling with her 16-year-old son after the boy got into some trouble at school. We were making pretty good progress with the boy until the day he got stopped by a police officer who found an open bottle of wine in the backseat. The mother reacted with such rage that she was still visibly upset six days after the incident, which was when they came to see me for their next appointment.

I met with both of them in my office, and things didn't go very well. At one point, her son asked her a direct question:

"Didn't you ever drink and drive at the same time?"

Mom acted like it was the dumbest question in the world. "Of course I didn't!"

It took all of my composure not to fall off my chair. I knew from previous sessions that this woman was an alcoholic. Surely she had driven while drinking at some point in her life.

I asked the son to leave the room for a few minutes, and then turned to his mother and asked, "Do you mean to say that you never operated a car when you were drinking or drunk?"

She waved her hand at me, as if to say my question was stupid.

"Of course I have. I've driven under the influence several times. But I certainly didn't want *him* to know that."

What a tragic mistake this mother had made. I hadn't been fooled by her lie and neither had her son. She had missed a golden opportunity to communicate with him at a level she had never reached before. If she had just had the courage to admit her mistakes, she might have been able to get her son to see how foolish it is to drink and drive. At the very least, she could have established new feelings of empathy and communication between them.

But instead she chose to play the ostrich—sticking her head in the sand, while her son and I saw her as she really was. I could make little progress with the boy after that session. He simply wasn't interested.

SHARE THE REAL YOU

My point is that if you want to communicate with your teenagers, you'd better be willing to be on the level with them. If you're not, they'll see right through it, and things will be worse than ever. If you are going to enter the private world of your teenager, you must be brave enough to be open and to relate some of the realities and complexities of your own life.

No, it's not easy. As you open up to your teenager you will have to go back to your own adolescent years and rekindle the thoughts, feelings, and experiences you had when you were in junior high and high school—and you may be surprised to find out that those were some pretty difficult days for you, even though the passage of time has painted them with a rosy, romantic glow. Not only that, but you're likely to be left with a bad case of nerves as you think, "Oh, no! My kid is going to do the same stupid things I did!"

Well, you may be right about that. But you got through it okay. And, it's just possible that by sharing with your children some of the mistakes you made, you will help them to avoid those same mistakes in their lives. At any rate, it is a much more effective approach than trying to convince your children that you were *always* perfect. They know better than that. In fact, chances are very good that your teenagers already know you better than you know yourself.

When children are small, they believe in just about everything anyone tells them. For example, I can remember when I was a boy, I was convinced that Roy Rogers was the king of the cowboys. Why? Because that's how he was billed. So Gene Autry was okay, and so were Hopalong Cassidy and the Lone Ranger—but they were all secondary to Roy . . . he was the king.

The same thing was true of Godzilla, who was billed as the king of the monsters. Rodan was cool. Mothra was okay. But Godzilla was king.

And I remember how my own kids used to believe every single advertising claim they heard on television—without reservation.

But when children reach the teenage years, they begin to discover that things are not always exactly as they are portrayed. The toy that looked so great on television, the one they just *had* to have, turns out to be a piece of junk. They find out that their movie hero has a stunt double. Santa Claus doesn't really exist.

And so they begin looking at everything with a critical eye (with the exception of their own peer group). That includes their Mom and Dad. They're watching you closely to see what you're really made of, to see if you do what you say, and if you always live up to the standards you say you hold.

They see it when you fail, but they're generally willing to be forgiving and understanding if you say, "Boy, I really goofed that time, didn't I? I'm sorry." If, on the other hand, they see that you, as a parent, will go to any lengths to protect your "image," then they will be likely to consider you to be hypocritical and discount your advice as being worthless.

Everyone makes mistakes. The key to a family is to have the people who are close to you still love you when you do —warts and all. You build that kind of love when you share your flaws openly with your children. They will not think less of you. On the contrary, they will be much more approachable and willing to listen to what you have to say.

I am often put on the spot as a counselor because people tend to think I have the answers to all of life's problems. One of the things I enjoy the most is going on radio and television talk shows to help husbands, wives, and parents with their problems. But on more than one occasion on national television I have admitted to a caller that I wasn't quite sure how to answer a particular question in the short time allotted to me.

I have had the same thing happen in seminars and workshops. I find that when I am brave enough to dig down deep into my own life and relate to the parents who have come to get help, they will in turn open up and pour out their hearts to me.

I have to admit, though, that it is tempting to play the role of "expert," even when I know that a pat answer or a few words of advice will not begin to get at the heart of the problem. There is a tendency on my part to want to uphold my "image," but it would be wrong for me to seek to do that by passing out glib, surfacey advice. As a practicing psychologist and author of several books on parenthood and marriage, I am also extremely sensitive as to how people view me and my family. At times I have this overwhelming feeling that everyone thinks my children and my marriage ought to be perfect. And the truth is that, as much as I love my wife and my children, there are no perfect marriages, or perfect children either. And if I tend to forget that from time to time, my wife and kids can bring me back to reality in a hurry.

My wife, Sande, is the sounding board in my life. Besides being everything I could ever want in a wife, she is my closest friend. And as such, she keeps me humble and very honest.

For example, I had been gone on a speaking engagement one weekend and came home to find the water trickling down the street from our garden hose. Now, when I am gone for three days, I really miss Sande and the children. But one thing that really can make me angry is to have the children play with the hose in front of the house and let the water run, especially in the summer. (In Tucson, where we live, water bills get high enough without letting several hundred gallons go floating down the street.)

So I stalked into the house. Were my first words full of joy and excitement because I had been reunited with my loved ones? Not quite. As I hit the hallway I roared, "Who left the water running in front of the house?"

From the kitchen came Sande's answer. "Oh, he's home, the family counselor."

It is strange how a few words from your wife can bring you down from your high horse (and your pedestal) in an instant. I put down my bags, went back outside, and did the necessary thing. I turned off the hose.

I share that little story with you to illustrate that all families have their moments of tension, and anyone can have his times of imperfection and shortcoming, no matter what kinds of letters appear after his name. I am glad that to my children I am just "Dad." I'm not a psychologist or Dr. Leman, or a Ph.D. I am just Dad and I am quite capable of saying the wrong thing and hurting tender, budding teenage feelings. I have been known, for example, to press one of my daughters as to how she feels about a certain "special" boy, when she would rather not talk about that just now. I have been known to speak first and think about it later. And, yes, there have been many times when I've had to use those two very important words: "I'm sorry," and the ever-popular, "I was wrong."

I have also come to see through firsthand experience that if I am to help my own kids get through the turbulent, wild waters called adolescence, I must be willing to take the first step to enter their private world. That means establishing a spirit of cooperation and equality.

I believe that parents can still be in charge, even as we allow our children to feel that spirit of equality that says we think they are important, that we have confidence in them and believe they can make intelligent decisions about life if we give them the chance.

So open up. Begin to allow your teenagers to see who you really are. Then and only then can you help them with the tough subjects: peer pressure, dating and sex, love, saying no to alcohol and drugs. We will talk about all of these things in the pages ahead, and I'll try to give you a few answers.

Bear in mind that I don't have all of the answers. Nobody does. But I do know the first rule: *Be real.* Your kids will love you for it—and maybe, just maybe, they will even listen to what you have to say.

1. Ronald L. Koteskey, "Growing Up Too Late Too Soon," *Christianity Today* (March 13, 1981), p. 24.

1

Is There an Adolescent in the House?

One of the things I've always admired about comedian Bill Cosby is his ability to see the humor in everyday situations, even those situations which really aren't all that funny—at least not while you're going through them.

In his popular movie concert of a few years back, *Bill Cosby, Himself,* he spends some time talking about what it's like to live in a house with four children.[1]

Among his candid observations: "People ask us why we had four children. We tell them it's because we didn't want any more!"

But to me, one of the funniest scenes in that concert is where Cosby explains what it's like eating dinner at the same table with his adolescent children, who are listening to up-tempo music while they eat, and eating to the beat of the music.

He goes through some hilarious gyrations as he shows how his kids move in time to the music, and then he stares straight down at the floor. "I don't look at 'em," he says.

In this one gesture, he gives vent to the feelings of parents of adolescents everywhere.

What's going on here? What are these kids doing? Are they nuts? Well, if I can't stop their behavior, at least I don't have to look at them while they're doing it.

As in, "Honey, did you see what your daughter wore to school this morning?"

"Uh, no . . . I was afraid to look."

"Welcome home, dear. Wait until you see your son's new haircut."

"Oh, no. Is it really bad? Do I have to see it before dinner?"

Something strange happens to kids when they hit adolescence. One day they're fine, and the next day they begin acting like they're newly arrived on this planet—and don't have a single clue as to how normal people are supposed to live.

One day, your son goes out of the house with a regular haircut, but comes home later looking like a strange mixture of Brian Bosworth, Don King, and Mr. T. Why did he cut his hair like that? Because he's an adolescent, that's why, and it's certainly a better excuse than any *he* could give you.

Or your daughter goes out in the morning in her new outfit, and comes home in the afternoon, wearing some clothes you've never seen before. When you ask here where *her* clothes are, you discover that she let Rhonda borrow her new sweater, and Jodi has her new jeans, and she left her top at Nicole's house. She, in turn, is wearing clothes she picked up at all of these girls' houses, and it's "good luck, Mom," trying to keep up with the mix-n-match clothing switcheroo. Why are adolescent girls always switching clothes with each other? Because they're adolescents, that's why. There's no other answer for it.

There are other changes that take place when a child becomes an adolescent. All of a sudden the kind who never got within six feet of a washcloth in his entire life now stands before a mirror scrubbing his face until it glistens; he shampoos and blow-dries his hair at least once a day, and sometimes more, seeking perfection.

The adolescent daughter takes a bath and leaves the water running continuously—with the stopper still in—so the "schmootz" floating on the water runs out through the overflow drain instead of sticking to her body.

This excessive concern with their physical appearance is tremendously burdensome for many teenagers because it's during their adolescent years that they encounter all kinds of physical problems: skin blemishes, lack of coordination, tongue-tiedness, and a disturbing emerging sexual awareness. Research substantiates the fact that sex drive is probably the greatest during those late teenage years of 16 to 18— especially for boys.

And wouldn't you know it, that you're most interested in the opposite sex just when you feel your ugliest and clumsiest, and just when all you have to do is think about chocolate and you're going to get a big zit right on the end of your nose.

One of my favorite cartoons is Gary Larson's "The Far Side," and one that I particularly enjoyed has a man standing in front of the mirror with a tree growing right out the top of his head. As he looks disgustedly at his reflection he says, "Wouldn't you know it! . . . And always just before a big date."[2]

To me, that cartoon sums up the plight that has been faced by many an adolescent boy or girl. That big zit may not be as obvious as a tree, but it certainly feels like it—and why does it always have to show up at exactly the wrong moment?

There are many negative factors which contribute to the adolescent's feelings about himself. And it's critical that we as parents understand that the poorer a teenager's self-esteem, the greater the impact of the peer group on his value system.

ADOLESCENTS WANT TO BE PERFECT

Can you imagine a big zit on Madonna's face? Or Michael Jackson falling over a crack in the sidewalk? Or M.C. Hammer looking awkward and clumsy on the dance floor?

It's no wonder adolescents don't have good feelings about themselves. Look at the models our world portrays to them —Tom Cruise, Michael Jackson, and Madonna—with these examples is it any wonder that adolescents are critical of themselves and others? Teenagers are great flaw-pickers. If an adolescent happens to be physically different—even in the least little way, then watch out. Things are going to get rough. And about the first sign that a kid is different is in the nickname other kids put on him.

Thinking about my own teenage years I remember some of the names we gave to the kids in our group: There was Moonhead, Jughead, Bellhead, and Craterhead. I was Craterhead. I happen to have two chicken pox scars on my forehead and one of my "friends" thought that was sort of funny. One evening he branded me "Craterhead." I tried to laugh it off, but it hurt. To this day I have never forgotten how it felt.

A friend of mine remembers that he was called "Tweetie Bird" because his friends thought his head was too big for his body.

Another friend has shared with me how she ate lunch outside all by herself every day during the eighth grade. She wouldn't even go into the cafeteria because she was afraid the other kids would tease her because they thought she was "different." And yet, every day when she went home and her parents would ask her how it went at school, she'd say "fine" because she didn't want them to worry about her.

If these kinds of things went on when we were kids, you can bet they're going on today. So don't try to patronize your children with statements like, "This is the best time of your life." In some ways that may be true—but in many other ways, life is going to get much better later on.

Adolescents are sensitive about their own differences, but they are critical and sometimes cruel to their peers who are different. I must admit that I was involved in giving the "girl with the flattest chest in the eighth grade" a pair of falsies for her thirteenth birthday. I flinch when I remember the young lady opening that gift at her party in front of all the kids. Most of the guys were gathered together in one corner, laughing and screaming and having a great time at her expense.

I remember the many times we used to choose ball teams, and more often than not the same kid in our neighborhood was the last one to be picked. I'm surprised that he came around as much as he did. After everyone else was chosen, it always got down to, "And Harold is on *your* team." After all, he did bring the ball and bat, which meant that he at least got to play—although his presence on your team was generally regarded as more of a liability than an asset.

But we certainly weren't kind to him if he dropped a ball or struck out.

I wonder if Harold looks back with fondness on those days. I doubt it.

Some people may sail right through adolescence and have a wonderful time while doing it—but those people are certainly very few and very far between.

Where do you suppose teenagers get the idea that anything less than perfection simply will not do? For one thing, they are bombarded daily with perfect models proclaiming the virtues of various products—from skin cleansers to soda pop. If your clothes don't have the right labels attached, you must be some kind of freak; if you don't drink the right soft drink you must be a dweeb, or geek, or whatever this week's latest derogatory term might be; if you don't listen to the right kind of music then you can't be part of the in-group, and so it goes.

Not only that, but those of us who claim to be part of the adult society enforce perfectionism in our own children. Why do we think our kids have to be the best at everything?

It's also true that our perfectionistic society isn't very tolerant of mistakes. Even teachers who have been trained to be sensitive to children have the audacity to write at the top of a test, "–3." What's wrong with a "+47" instead? We often choose to say things in negative terms, when positive terms would get the message across in a much better way. Too often we have become a society of flaw-pickers, and this is not good for our children, nor for any of the rest of us for that matter.

Have you ever had the experience of sitting in a musical concert at your child's school, when all of a sudden the kid playing the clarinet hit a note that had never been heard before in all of recorded history? A note that everyone present hopes they never hear again?

I'm sure you have. Well, what kind of feelings went through you when you heard that child make a mistake? Did your heart pound? Did you become very uncomfortable and have to avert your eyes to avoid showing how embarrassed you were for him? My point is that everyone makes mistakes, but as a society we've become too good at thinking in terms of perfection, and reinforcing perfectionist notions in our children's minds. We must be careful that we don't expect our kids to be perfect, or plant in their minds the notion that they have to be perfect. We as parents need to know two very important truths, and teach them to our children. They are:

1. Nobody is perfect.
2. Everybody makes mistakes.

So cut yourself, and your adolescent, some slack!

ADOLESCENTS FEEL INFERIOR

James Dobson said it best in his book *Preparing for Adolescence*. He refers to the "canyon of inferiority."[3] If there's one thing that characterizes adolescents it's that feeling of inferiority—that awkward feeling that makes a young boy or girl think that nobody else in the world is as ugly as he is, as clumsy as he is, has as many pimples as he does, etc. Of course, it doesn't help his adolescent ego when the 14-year-old male answers the phone and the person on the other end of the line says, "Hello, young lady, is your mother home?" or when the caller asks the boy, "Is this Mrs. Johnson?"

Adolescents usually are masters of the put-down, and the primary reason for this is that they feel so inferior themselves. A child of 12 or 13 or older may make cutting remarks regarding everything and everyone because he doesn't feel good about himself. He can't see anything good within himself, so he refuses to see anything good in anything else.

19

Probably the most common statement I hear from parents of teenagers or younger adolescents is that they just don't understand what has happened to their child. Just last week Snooky was so sweet and cooperative and loving. Now she's irritable, cantankerous, volatile—totally unpredictable.

The reason for this, too, is that her self-esteem is probably at an all-time low. When everything seems to be going wrong, when things seem to be piling up emotionally, many teenagers choose to strike out. And you know who the target is going to be. Those who are within range, including Mom and Dad, brother and sister.

The child's thinking is along the lines of, "Okay, life is being unfair to me, so I have the right to let somebody have it."

There are several reasons why kids at this age suffer from such low self-esteem. For one thing, because this is the time when a boy is likely to grow six or seven inches in a single year, he's likely to be especially clumsy as he adjusts to his new body. Suddenly, his feet have become huge clownlike things, and he has trouble putting one of them in front of the other without tripping. This is also the time for braces, and the ever-popular zits.

It's especially tough for boys because they have noticed the girls their own age in a big way. But those girls have noticed the boys who are two or three years older, some of whom actually own their own cars. And it's especially tough for the girls, because most of them can't get the older boys to pay the least bit of attention to them. It's a vicious circle!

But not all of the adolescents' feelings of inferiority are brought on by such things. I believe that we parents, as a group, have to take much of the blame for the frustrations these growing-up children feel.

Most parents today, I believe, have done a beautiful job of

snowplowing the roads for their children, and that's not good. We are like the king's attendants who have to walk before him, spreading his path with rose petals. It's all because we want the best for our children, but it winds up being hurtful instead of helpful, because it doesn't allow them to make their own decisions—to "stand up on their own two feet" and discover for themselves what works and what doesn't work in life. It doesn't allow them the joy of discovering that with effort and determination they *can* and *will* succeed in life—and that they can do so on their own.

Now when I start talking this way in one of my seminars, it's just about certain that someone is going to interrupt me in mid-sentence. "Hold on just a minute. My wife and I know what's best for our children, and that's why we've set up some rules and regulations that we expect them to follow— no matter how they feel about it."

What's my response to this? "That's fine. But what I'm trying to point out is that if you don't give your child some freedom to make his own choices, you are setting him up for all kinds of problems. And when he faces the most important decisions of his life, he may not be able to make the right choices." No parent can make those decisions for his children. Yes, you can lay the foundation so that your child's choices are likely to be the right ones. You should always be there to offer your suggestions and guidance, and you should provide the proper training so that he knows what's right and what's wrong. But the rest is up to him. You cannot live your child's life for him, no matter how tempting it might be to try.

During my 14-year tenure as assistant dean of students at the University of Arizona, I saw thousands of freshmen come and go. Some of them came into town, looked around them, and said something like, "I'm free! Let's party!" And party they did. They drank gallons of beer, they smoked as much pot as they could score, they pursued the freshmen of the opposite sex with tremendous enthusiasm.

Some of them never made it through the first semester. Some were jolted back to reality by their first semester's grades, and others quickly tired of the party scene and settled in to college life. But what was most interesting to me was the discovery that most of those who really went off the deep end came from homes where they had never had to make choices for themselves.

Mom and Dad had said, "This is the way it's going to be as long as you live in this house. We'll tell you what to do, and we expect you to do it, no questions asked." These were good, moral homes, where everything looked great to anyone looking in from the outside, but they were homes in which the children received no training in life's realities.

Some of these kids had parents who were not only authoritarian in their approach to parenting, but parents who covered for them at every opportunity, who had never let them make choices, good or bad, and then reap the benefits or suffer the consequences of those choices. In other words, these kids had been stifled and overprotected, and now they were going to stretch those young wings and fly. Never mind that many of them didn't have the slightest idea *how* to fly.

When I think of parents who allowed their children to make their own choices, with terrific results, I think of the mother of a girl named Ginny. Ginny was a beautiful young lady of 17. Her blond hair and blue eyes were accompanied by a trim figure and a neat, outgoing personality. She was a cheerleader and student body officer at her high school. Everybody seemed to like her and even though, by her own admission, she was the only virgin on the cheerleading squad, she never lacked for male attention.

22

She also was blessed with a good relationship with her mother, and the two of them could talk about everything. Frequently, after a Friday or Saturday evening date, Ginny and her mother would stay up until past 2:00 A.M., talking about everything from that evening's date to some of the more controversial issues of the day.

One Friday afternoon Ginny came home and told her mother that she wanted to go to a party, a party "everybody" was going to. It was the biggest event of the school year, and Ginny wanted to be dropped off at the house where the party was being held. She also told her mother that she was a little bit concerned about this party because she thought there might be some drinking and pot smoking there. But nevertheless, she still wanted to go very badly.

It would have been easy for Ginny's mother to say, "You're not going to any party where there's going to be drinking and marijuana. No way. You're just going to stay home." But instead, she did a very brave thing. She told her daughter that it was her decision to make, and if she wanted to go then, yes, she would drive her over and drop her off.

In spite of her many reservations, Ginny still wanted to go. She figured the pluses definitely outweighed any minuses that might be involved.

So Mom drove her daughter to the party, but just before dropping her off she said, "Listen—I'm going to be waiting down the street about half a block. I'll be there for 15 minutes or so. If things are not what you think they should be, feel free to come on out and I'll give you a ride home."

Well, you guessed what happened. Mom waited about 10 minutes before she saw her daughter heading down the sidewalk toward the car. "Mom, I couldn't handle it," she said. "It was a zoo. There were a lot of older people there—

kids from other schools and university students as well—drinking and smoking and acting crazy. I want to go home."

I think someone should have pinned a medal on Ginny's mom for her bravery and wisdom in handling the situation in just the right way. What a brave, wise, and loving woman! She knew what was best for her daughter, and it would have been very easy to just say no. But she gave the girl the right to make her own decision. One of the reasons why Ginny's mom could give her that decision-making opportunity was because she and her husband had always given their daughter plenty of chances to make her own choices. So even though this was a more sophisticated and dangerous choice than she had ever made before, she had plenty of practice as a youngster in making decisions.

What is your adolescent going to say when someone offers him a joint? And rest assured that someone *will* offer him a joint.

Is he going to think, "No, my folks wouldn't let me smoke pot?" No way. But if he's used to making his own decisions, he may turn it down because he reasons that "I don't want it because I know it isn't good for me. I don't want to do anything that would make me lose control, or that could get me in trouble with the law."

You can't be looking over Johnny's shoulder all the time, saying, "No, no . . . don't you drink that beer." Or, "Don't you dare light up that marijuana cigarette." Or, "Johnny, don't you even think about having sex with that girl!"

But you can teach him early in life the importance of making good solid decisions, so that he'll understand why he's too young to have a few beers, why he ought to stay away from marijuana and other drugs, and why sex is not to be viewed simply as another form of recreation.

Not only is it important that children have the opportunity to make their own choices, but it's also important that, when those choices are bad ones, they be given the opportunity to suffer the consequences, and thereby learn from their mistakes.

Now I realize that this type of thinking gets me into trouble with a lot of softhearted parents. They don't want to see anything happen that might damage little Hurkimer's psyche. But failure can be an excellent teacher. There's something to be said for "the school of hard knocks."

Suppose, for instance, that it's Thursday night, and your son comes to you and says, "Uh . . . I've got a science project due tomorrow."

"A science project? How long have you known about this."

"Oh, maybe three weeks."

"Three weeks? And you're just now telling me about it?"

"Well, I'm sorry . . . but I've had so many other things to do and then . . . you know . . . I kind of . . . you know . . . forgot."

"Forgot? Have you started it yet? Have you done anything at all."

"Er . . . well . . . you know . . . not really."

And so there you have a major problem. How are you going to handle it? If you're like most parents, you'll probably drop everything else you're doing, sit down at the dining room table with the kid, and spend the rest of the evening trying to come up with something that will at least net him a passing grade.

But when it's all over, what has the boy learned from the experience? Nothing at all, except that the next time he screws things up, good old Mom or Dad will come along and bail him out, just like this time. Oh, you may yell at him a little bit, and tell him that he's got to do a better job of keeping on top of things—but the kid figures that he can live with a little bit of yelling.

What he needs to have happen is for you to say, "You have a science project due tomorrow, and you haven't even started it? Sounds to me like you'd better get busy."

"But I can never get it done in time now."

"I'm sorry, but this is your problem. There's not a thing I can do about it."

It sounds cruel, perhaps, but in reality it is anything *but* cruel. It's teaching the child to be responsible for his own actions. He'll have to face the humiliation of admitting to his teacher that he goofed around and didn't get the project done. He'll have to bear the brunt of the bad grade in the class, and the next time a major project is assigned, chances are very good that he will start on it in plenty of time to get it finished by the deadline.

If you study the lives of great people, you'll find that almost all of them were very well acquainted with failure. It can be a great boost toward future success.

ADOLESCENTS WANT TO BE LIKE EVERYBODY ELSE

Regarding Ginny and the party, I believe one of the reasons she was able to make such a wise choice where other adolescents might not have is because her mother's confidence in her gave her the strength to be different, to resist going along with the crowd when she knew it was wrong.

Teenagers are under a great deal of pressure to conform, to be like everyone else in their accepted peer group. And what the peer group likes is usually not going to be anything at all similar to what Mom and Dad like. As a matter of fact, if the old folks like something there must be something wrong with it, so the kids have to toss it on the junk pile.

That reminds me of the 16-year-old boy who was buying a shirt in a department store. As the sales clerk was ringing up his purchase, he asked, "Excuse me . . . but if my parents like this shirt, can I bring it back?"

Teenagers seem to go out of their way to be "in"—and if some fashion guru declared that boys were supposed to start wearing dresses and girls were supposed to start wearing slacks and shirts, I believe they'd follow his lead without question. As long as everybody else is doing it, then they'll do it too.

Of course, we are all subject to peer pressure, especially with regard to the dictates of fashion. Ties get skinny and then they get wide again. Hem lines go up, and then they go down. Lapels go from wide to thin and back to wide. Subdued colors are in, and then all of a sudden bright colors are the thing to wear. Skirts are straight, and then they're full. Pant legs are straight, and then it's bell-bottoms all the way. I will even admit to you that I was among the first men in my neighborhood to buy a leisure suit, back about 1974.

Think about what's popular in music. Is it rock, rap, or something new? And what about the fads that come and go —from goldfish swallowing to streaking to . . . well, who knows what will be going on five years from now? But something definitely *will* be going on, and just about everybody will be doing it. (Let's just hope it's not too expensive, fattening, or doesn't make us all look *too* ridiculous!)

Now if you want some more evidence regarding the power of peer pressure, let me tell you about an experiment that was conducted by a major university.

Several hundred people were recruited to help scientists study the ability of people to make simple judgments based on their perceptions. At least, that's what the people were told. Actually, the whole thing was to see if people would give in to peer pressure, even when their eyes told them that what everyone else was saying was wrong.

The volunteers were divided into groups of ten, taken into separate rooms, and shown three sentences via an overhead projector. Then, they were simply asked to raise their hands as to which sentence was the longest. "How many of you think that the first sentence is the longest? Okay . . . how many pick the second sentence?" And so on. In every situation, it was the third sentence that was actually the longest.

Now nine out of every ten "volunteers" were in on a little secret. They were all going to vote for the second sentence, even though it was obviously shorter by several words. The idea was to see if the tenth person would go along with the group, even though he should be able to see clearly that the group was wrong.

That is exactly what happened. Time after time, when that tenth person looked around the room and saw all those other hands in the air, he put his hand up too. Only one-fourth of those tested were actually brave enough to go against the tide of public opinion, to say, "Hey, I don't know what the rest of you think you see up there, but that third sentence is obviously the longest of the three."

Now this experiment wasn't conducted solely on adolescents, but if it had been, I'm quite certain that the percentage of conformity would have been closer to 100 percent. That's because as strong as the pull of peer pressure is on the rest of us, it's two or three times stronger on adolescents, beginning with preteens and carrying right on through to young adulthood.

I mentioned earlier my days at the University of Arizona. During that time I was in charge of code of conduct and discipline. There were some fun parts to that job and some not-so-fun parts.

But one of the things I enjoyed most of all was registration time every year, and especially watching the new students come onto the university campus. The first few days a freshman could be spotted a mile a way. He would be the one who seemed to be wandering around in a stupor, looking up at the tall buildings, bumping into palm trees, and asking stupid questions like, "Excuse me, but could you tell me where the TBA building is?" "TBA" means "to be announced" and it's found in the schedule of classes. It's a very typical question for a college freshman to ask.

But after a couple of weeks, even those of us who claim to be experts in the area of students on campus find it very difficult to pick out the freshmen. Why? Because they have quickly learned what is expected of them by way of the peer group and they blend in. Their dress, demeanor, language, even the way they walk is dictated by the peer group. Peer pressure is alive and well, even on a college campus where students are quick to point out how individualistic and free of family restraints they are.

If you get peer pressure moving in the right direction, it can be a terrific force for good. But get it rolling down a negative slope and watch out, because it can lead toward rebellion and anarchy—as it almost did in the late sixties and early seventies.

ADOLESCENTS ARE SEXUALLY AWARE

Let me tell you something that may shock you a bit about your sweet and innocent little Johnnie and Joannie. They may be sweet, but they're not innocent—especially when it

29

comes to sex. I'm not saying they're sexually active, and I certainly hope that they're not, but they know all about sex.

Sexual awareness is a very natural part of adolescence, even though most kids are woefully ill-prepared to deal with the changes that are taking place within their bodies.

Ronald L. Koteskey says that today's teenagers are facing sexual frustrations that were not faced by people of a century or more ago, and I believe he's right.[4]

I have found out that there are two words that many adults don't really handle very well. The first one of those words is *sex* and the second is *masturbation.*

Regarding the first one, I was in Chicago one time and thought I'd call a bookstore to see if they were carrying a copy of a book I had written. A woman clerk answered the phone and I asked, "Do you have *Sex Begins in the Kitchen?*" There was a shocked silence on the other end of the line, and then she literally screamed into the phone, "Where I have sex is none of your business!" And she hung up on me. I have to admit that I didn't have the courage to call her back. All she heard was the word "sex" and she had immediately tuned me out.

There are many reasons why most of us have tuned out the word "masturbation." One reason is that the term itself comes from two Latin words that mean "to pollute with the hand." It doesn't even sound like a nice thing to do, does it? But one thing you can pretty much count on is the fact that your adolescent is going to do it. When I was young we used to say that 90 percent of the guys masturbated, and the other 10 percent were liars.

You may remember the old joke in which you'd sidle up to a friend and say, "Did you know that half the people in the world masturbate while they're in the shower, and the other half sing?"

"No, I didn't."

"Yeah, and those who sing all sing the same song. Do you know which song it is?"

"Uh . . . no . . . what is it?"

"Hah . . . you don't know the song. Well now we know what *you* do in the shower."

Well, it was funny, way back then.

But my point is that masturbation is engaged in by almost all teenage boys and the vast majority of teenage girls—and in my opinion there is absolutely nothing wrong with that. It is a harmless way to release sexual tension and to begin to come to terms with one's sexual identity.

Unfortunately, too many of us have come to think of masturbation as something that's dirty and evil, and we've passed those feelings along to our children. That doesn't mean they're going to stop masturbating, just that they're going to feel guilty about it when they do.

I'm sure you remember some of the things that used to be said about masturbation. It would cause hair to grow on the palms of your hands. It would cause you to go crazy. It would make you become sterile.

Well, none of those things are true, and if you suspect that your adolescent might be engaging in masturbation, the only thing I can tell you is that he's perfectly normal sexually.

Masturbation is simply one way adolescents can safely, and without harm to themselves or anyone else, relieve their sexual pressures. Most of the adolescents I talk to tell me that their parents did not really talk to them about sex, and teenage boys have not been prepared for the eventuality of a nocturnal emission—or a wet dream. A young male will have wet dreams in the absence of masturbation during the adolescent years. It's a very natural way for the boy's body to rid itself of extra semen. Can you imagine how guilty a young

31

man might feel if he had a wet dream and he had not been prepared for the experience by either parent.

One such boy told me that when it happened to him, he knew he had done something terrible, and had probably "broken" his penis. "I didn't know what had happened, but I figured that whatever it was, it wasn't something that was *supposed* to happen," he told me. As time went by and it became apparent that everything was "working normally," he felt a tremendous sense of relief.

Although parents in some circles have made a big fuss over masturbation, it is really just part of a person's development. The only problem I have seen with regard to it is that some people may become overly preoccupied with it. When that happens, it can contribute to an unhealthy fantasy life and feelings of guilt or lust. To help keep masturbation under control, kids need to avoid sexually stimulating movies, television programs, books, magazines, music, etc., as much as possible. They should also find other outlets such as athletics, strenuous work, or hobbies for releasing the emotional tension caused by their sexual drives. Masturbation is a personal matter, but it is something each family needs to talk about. Kids have to make a determination concerning masturbation based on their own feelings and experiences.

I know it's not easy to talk about things like masturbation and sex, but for the sake of your children, parents, you really need to do it.

I'll tell you how it works in most families. Dad figures, "I suppose I ought to talk to the boy about the birds and bees." He calls his son into the den and says, "Harold, I think it's about time you and I had a man-to-man talk. Uh . . . so here's a little booklet I want you to read. And after you've read it, if you have any questions, maybe you can call me at the office some time. Well . . . it's been great talking to you, son."

Maybe I'm exaggerating it, but then again, maybe I'm not. But your children need more than a booklet. They need for you to share with them on a heart-to-heart level, and for your availability to answer any questions they might have.

I will never forget the first time I talked to my oldest daughter, Holly, about sex. I was tucking her into bed one night, when she was about 10, and she began asking me some very direct questions—to which I gave her some very direct replies. I didn't get too far before she wrinkled her nose and said, "How *gross.*" End of discussion. Holly is now in college, and I hope that she still has that attitude about sex. As far as I'm concerned, she can start getting serious about "boys" when she hits 30. (Now you see I've gone from being a psychologist to being a protective father!)

What I'm saying here is that when your kids start asking questions, do your best to answer them as honestly and as thoroughly as you can. And don't think that you've done your job when you've discussed the mechanics of sex.

When you talk about sex, you also need to talk about love and commitment. You might want to share with your children how you and your spouse met, how you fell in love, when you decided to get married. You can share with them how happy you were when you discovered that you were going to be parents.

If your child seems shy and awkward in his dealings with the opposite sex, it will do him good to hear that you were the same way at one time. Did you have an embarrassing "dating" experience when you were just venturing out into the world of "male-female relationships"? Tell him or her about that too.

And then, of course, you need to tell him that there are

several reasons why sex is not to be engaged in lightly, and why it is, in fact, better to view it as something that should take place only between one man and one woman who are married to each other.

Here are some things to teach your adolescents about sex.

1. It's okay to say no. It doesn't mean you're a nerd or a wimp, but it does mean that you respect and value your own body, and that you also respect and value the bodies of others.

2. Sex causes pregnancy, even in these days of readily available birth control devices. The only birth control measure that is 100 percent effective is abstinence. An unwanted pregnancy hurts the mother, the child, and everyone else who becomes involved in the situation.

3. There is something powerful about sex. It causes two people to think they are "in love" when the reality may be that they don't have a single thing in common. Many a young person has found himself trapped in a loveless and angry marriage because he mistook sex for love.

4. Sex precludes intimacy. Once sex enters into a relationship it takes over. It is not a way of allowing you to get to know someone better. In fact, it can get in the way of getting to know someone better.

5. Sex can lead to AIDS, venereal disease, and potentially other health problems. For example, a girl who is sexually active at a young age and who has numerous partners is more likely to develop cancer of the cervix.

6. There is something very special about knowing that you and your mate have never been with anyone else—that neither one of you has given yourself to anyone else as completely as you have given yourself to each other.

We're going to talk more about teenagers and sex in Chapter 3, but before we move on I want to say one other thing on the subject.

That is that I believe it's the mother who should talk to her sons about sex, and the father who should talk to his daughters. I know this flies in the face of conventional wisdom. But the fact is that it's the opposite-sex parent who has the most profound effect on the children.

Father, your daughters need to know from your perspective how men feel about women—good and bad. They need to hear from you how much you love their mother, to see that men are capable of tenderness and love.

Mother, your boys need the same from you. They need to understand that girls have sexual feelings just like boys do and, most of all, that they are real people with real feelings who deserve to be treated with gentleness and respect. Teach your sons, Mom, that girls are not sex objects to be "conquered" and then cast aside, but that there is a special young woman out there right now for him to love, treasure, and commit himself to.

It's important, Mom, that you don't take any guff from your teenage son. If you let him push you around, he's going to think he can push all women around. The relationship he has with you is the model for all of his future relationships with women.

The same is true of your daughters, Dad. Treat them lovingly, gently, and with respect. Let them see that you treat their mother the same way. I have counseled dozens of women who were married to abusive men, and in almost every instance the whole problem started because when she was a little girl she did not have a good relationship with her father. He may not have been abusive, but he certainly was not a good influence in her life, and she is still paying the price for it.

One of my favorite newspaper columnists is Erma Bombeck, who wrote a column in which she cited a Duke University survey which says that 30 percent of American teenagers have engaged in sexual intercourse by the time they are 15. She wrote:

"There isn't a person in the world who will admit (if he is honest) that he is the same person after his first sexual experience that he was before. He left something behind that was so special even he didn't realize it. Some call it innocence. I'm not sure it has a name. But whatever it is, it's impossible to recapture it again. Even if you are married, the relationship changes.

"Age knows what youth has not yet learned—that there is time. There are patches of life that follow a pattern of growth. There's a time for discovery, a time for adventure, a time to be a child, a time to learn, a time to find your place. Don't even try to fast-forward it. Enjoy every minute. You get only one chance to be 15."[5]

To that I can only add, "Amen."

ADOLESCENTS LONG FOR FREEDOM

Someone asked me not too long ago, "How do you really know when your child begins adolescence?" The only really surefire way to know is to be sensitive to the first time your 11- or 12-year-old sinks down into the car seat as you drive past some kids on the corner. If he does that, then he's reached adolescence.

An adolescent is embarrassed by his parents—and that's

no reflection on his mom and dad, it's just the way it is.

You may remember the words of Mark Twain, who said that when he was a teenager he thought his father was ignorant, but by the time he had grown up he was amazed at how much the old man had learned in the intervening years. Well, an adolescent may not think his mother and father are ignorant, but he sure doesn't want to be *seen* with them. He doesn't want his friends to think that his parents are "in charge" of his life. And he himself wants to be "free," even though he is still very much dependent upon his parents.

Ask a child sometime, "What age would you be if you could be any age at all?" The typical answer to that question is 16. Why? What's so special about 16? Well, for one thing, they know they can drive at that age, and that's a biggy. Driving represents independence. In the teenager's life today the car is certainly very close to being number one. That's one reason why, when counseling parents of adolescents, I suggest that when it comes to discipline they zero in on three things: the car, money, and privileges. These are three things that the American teenager relates to almost without exception. If he realizes that his actions are going to have a negative impact in any of those areas, then he'll at least think twice before engaging in those actions.

Now even though an adolescent longs for his freedom, he's anything but free. He has parents who tell him what to do. He may have younger brothers and sisters who drive him up the wall, or older brothers and sisters who boss him around. He has teachers who don't understand and give him assignments that are either boring or much too difficult. He has demands put onto him by the peer group—and he sometimes feels the need to go along with the crowd, whether or not he really wants to.

This lack of freedom is one reason why some teenagers rebel.

Kelly, who was 15 when I first met her, is a case in point.

She came to me at the suggestion of her parents, who were concerned about the changes they were seeing in their daughter. Kelly's mom was a home-ec teacher, a perfectionist, a rather high-strung woman, and very overprotective of her daughter. She was president of the local PTA, and had some very definite ideas about child rearing. Those ideas seemed to have worked very well with her two older children, but not with Kelly, who was the baby of the family. The oldest boy was in law school, while the other boy was a college freshman. Both of them seemed to be well-adjusted, good citizens who were headed for success in life. But not Kelly.

Kelly's dad was an easygoing, laid-back professional person, a dentist with a very heavy work load. He was good at keeping his emotions to himself. Kelly didn't worry very much about him because he didn't get upset about things. But it was another story with her mother. Kelly told me that she thought her whole life had been mapped out for her by her mother, that her mom knew exactly what she should be when she got older, what to study, who to date, and what to wear.

Kelly's parents' concern for the girl was justified. Her mother told me, "She's bright, outgoing, an excellent student. But she is also lazy, self-centered, and manipulative. She has recently begun cutting classes at school."

At 14, Kelly had shown an inordinate desire to be with young men. She started dating older guys, over her parents' objections. They tried to stop it, but finally decided that it wasn't worth the constant hassles and gave in on the subject.

Kelly had begun a quick downward slide as her fifteenth birthday approached. She became rebellious to the point of being openly defiant. Out of the blue she displayed a smart mouth, as well as language that wasn't fit for the saltiest of sailors. Mom (and remember, she was the president of the PTA) started to get a series of calls from the school. Not only was Kelly's ditching increasing, but she would show up at school drunk (when she bothered to come to school at all) in her 8:30 morning class. Her parents sought professional help for her when school officials caught her in the backseat of a car making out with a 19-year-old student.

As I met with her in therapy, it became very clear that there was no way Mom was going to control her life. She was going to show her folks that she was no longer the little girl they wanted her to be. She described her parents as terribly overprotective, archaic, old-fashioned, unrealistic, and boring. She said she was the only one of her friends who had a midnight curfew on weekends. Her whole lifestyle seemed to say that she counted in life only when she controlled, when she won, and when she was able to boss her parents around.

I admit there were times during our sessions when I felt helpless, due to Kelly's great desire to be the opposite of what her mother wanted her to be. And as far as Mom was concerned, she was not very good at following my advice to back off and give the girl some room.

Kelly finally decided that she was going to show her . . . and show her she did, but at what expense! The girl began a pattern of staying out past her curfew. The more she rebelled, the more Mom and Dad tried to clamp down, and finally one night she just didn't come home at all.

Then she left home "for good." She was gone for a period of about 13 months. Of course she was forced to quit school. During this time she lost almost all contact with her school friends and found a new group with which to associate— some crusty-looking fellows who didn't work regularly and rode motorcycles for enjoyment.

During those 13 months, Kelly was transformed from a relatively naive and sweet young lady into a hard and abused young woman. She went, in short order, from drinking a few beers a day to smoking so much pot that—in her own words—she was so wasted she could hardly see straight.

She finally moved in with three young men, ages 19 to 22, and shared a one-bedroom apartment with them. During this time she had many sexual experiences, not only with the three men she lived with, but with several others as well. She was used in the truest sense of the word. During that time she became pregnant twice, ended both of those pregnancies via abortion, and the last guy she "went with" left town as soon as he heard he was going to be a father. He was a coke-head and had already fathered two children at the age of 21, so it was just as well for Kelly that he *didn't* want to marry her.

After her 13 months of "freedom" Kelly began to make some overtures about coming home. She called me at my office one day, catching me totally by surprise. I was with a client, but took the time to speak with her when I learned who it was on the phone. She wanted to see me, so we set up an appointment for that afternoon.

When she walked into the office I could hardly believe my eyes. Where had the blond-haired, blue-eyed, pretty little 15-

year-old gone? What I saw before me now was frightening. She looked rough, beaten-down, and her language was atrocious. It was immediately obvious that she had very little left in the way of self-respect. I asked her flat-out if she had had enough of freedom and was ready to go home. As she sat in my office sobbing, she nodded her head; she wanted me to call her mom and dad.

That's what I did, they came to the office, and the four of us spent the afternoon talking about many of the same issues we had talked about a year earlier: responsibilities, curfews, language, smoking, drinking, pot-smoking, and her general demeanor. We began to work out an agreement that both parties could agree to.

It was a great personal joy for me to see Kelly want to go home and live with her parents. After all, they were the two people who loved her most in all this world. As I saw them leave the office that afternoon, arm-in-arm, I knew it wasn't going to be easy. It was going to be a very difficult process to put things back together and to heal a relationship that had been so badly broken. It's never easy for parents to forgive a child who they think has betrayed them, but Kelly's parents loved her enough that they were at least willing to make the effort.

In the months and years after Kelly went back home, I spent quite a bit of time with her, talking about how special she is and about her need to treat herself as special if she was ever going to be in a position to attract people who were good for her. Soon after she returned home I asked her, "If you could tell teenagers one thing, what would it be?"

Her response: "First, try to realize that even though your parents seem out of it they really do love you and care about what happens to you; second, stick it out at home no matter

41

how bad it is. Living out there in the world by yourself is the pits."

Perhaps you're thinking that Kelly is an extreme case. Let me assure you that she isn't. I have numerous case histories that are very similar to Kelly's, with many of the same hurts, trials, tribulations, and basically the same results. Given time, teenagers learn that there isn't a better place on earth than home.

Kelly was one angry and resentful young lady who wanted her freedom from a mom who had to make all her decisions for her. Fortunately, for all of them, Kelly came home and they had a second chance. She had learned that she needed her parents. And her mom had learned to love her daughter with open arms. She had learned to walk the tightrope between giving Kelly the love and guidance she needed, and giving her enough freedom to grow.

TAKE ACTION

Let's recap some of the traits of adolescents that we've discussed in this chapter.

Adolescents:

- Want to be perfect.
- Feel inferior.
- Are subject to incredible pressures from their peer group.
- Are sexually aware.
- Long for freedom.

Here are a couple of things you can do to help your adolescent cope with these situations and feelings:

• Try to set aside at least 15 minutes every night to talk to your child, to get to know what's on his mind. Don't structure it so much that he sees it as something you view as a "duty" or a "job." One night you might want to spend 15 minutes immediately after dinner, and another night 15 minutes right before bedtime. Ask him what's on his mind, and give him the chance to honestly express himself and, just as importantly, share yourself with him. Tell him about some of the ways you've goofed, some of the occasions when you felt inferior, etc. It will be a comfort to him to know that you've been along the same path he's walking today, and that you came out all right. Don't see this as a time when you have to accomplish anything, but rather as a way to keep the lines of communication open. That's very important, especially now.

• If you've never done it, call a family meeting and go over the rules of the family, asking for your adolescent's input as you do. Let him know that you'll listen to him and consider changing it if there's a particular rule he doesn't like. Hopefully, you can explain to him why some rules are too important to be changed. The whole process of discussing things with him will make him feel that you respect him, and also will reinforce the idea that you are allowing him a certain amount of "freedom." Your adolescent needs to know specifically what the ground-rules of the family are—what you expect of him and what's going to happen if he doesn't obey those rules.

• If you haven't done it, talk to your adolescents about sex. And remember, ideally, fathers should talk to daughters and mothers to sons. And as far as I'm concerned, no talk about sex is complete unless it also includes some words about love, respect, commitment, and marriage. Do your best to teach your children that sex is a beautiful thing, and that there's nothing wrong or dirty about it at all. But teach them, also, that it is a beautiful thing that has its place, and that place is between a man and woman who have pledged their lives to each other.

1. Bill Cosby, *Bill Cosby, Himself,* Twentieth Century Fox (1981).
2. Gary Larson, "The Far Side," Universal Press Syndicate (1990).
3. James Dobson, *Preparing for Adolescence* (Ventura, Calif.: Vision House Publishers 1978).
4. Koteskey, "Growing Up Too Late Too Soon," p. 24.
5. Erma Bombeck column, Universal Press Syndicate (August 8, 1991).

2

It Takes Guts to Be Different

A friend of mine recently returned from the twenty-year reunion of his high school class. He hadn't been able to attend the tenth because he lived too far away, so this was the first time he had seen many of his old classmates since graduation day.

He told me that he had a great time at the reunion, but that he had made one startling discovery. That was this: Most of the guys who had been considered "nerds" in high school—well, actually, they were called "dorks" back then—had done very well for themselves.

These were the guys who had walked around the halls carrying briefcases, who had pen-guards in their shirt pockets, who weren't afraid to be seen actually studying in study hall, and who were rarely seen without their slide rules. In short, they were "different" from everybody else, and the other kids tended to make fun of them because of it.

My friend said, "There were several of these guys in our class . . . and now they all have great jobs, they're driving expensive cars . . . and you should see some of the women these guys are married to. There wasn't a good-looking girl

45

in our class who would as much as give one of these guys the time of day—and they all have beautiful wives! It blew me away."

I'll bet it did.

My friend also told me that he told his son about his experiences at the reunion. He hoped it would help the boy to see that the key to success does not lie in going along with the crowd, but in daring to be different. He also wanted the boy to understand that the things that are most likely to attract a high school girl—a killer car, a cool haircut, and the ability to throw or catch a touchdown pass—are not likely to be the same things that attract a mature woman, but he wasn't quite sure he was getting through to the boy.

Perhaps not, because the truth is that it takes guts, and plenty of them, for an adolescent to refuse to conform.

To what extent will young people go to be accepted by the group? Well, have you ever asked your adolescent, "If all the other kids were jumping off the Empire State Building would you do it too?" (I know it's a dumb question, but parents have been saying it ever since that building went up in the center of Manhattan. It's almost come to be expected of us.) Your son or daughter says, "Of course not . . . I'm not *stupid*."

But I want to tell you something. I've seen enough of the results of peer pressure that I'm just about convinced that if everyone in his peer group were jumping off the Empire State Building, the average adolescent would be right up there with them, getting ready to do the old 1100-foot cannonball onto the sidewalk below.

I once worked with a young man who had done a 180-degree turn in school. He'd gone from being an *A* student to failing almost all of his classes, and he'd done it in almost no time at all. What had happened to him? Peer pressure, pure and simple. He had been treated as an outcast by the other kids because of his outstanding grades, and he had decided that it was more important to him to be a part of the group than it was to do well in school.

Can you think back to a time in elementary school when you knew the right answer to a question the teacher asked but didn't put your hand up? Why didn't you? For one thing, you were afraid of that one chance in a million that you might be wrong, and you didn't want to look silly in front of the other kids. And then, too, part of the reason might have been that you didn't want the other kids to think you were a know-it-all or a show-off.

If you're like most of us, you can probably remember sitting in a class and not really understanding what the teacher was getting at. Perhaps it was a math or science class—something complicated that was hard to grasp the first time through. The teacher finished his discussion and said, "Okay now . . . are there any questions? If there's anything you don't understand about this, please ask me and I'll go over it again."

You had about 10 questions running through your mind . . . but you looked around the room and not a single hand went up. "Well," you thought, "if none of them have any questions to ask, then I'm not going to raise my hand, either. I'm not going to look stupid."

That's peer pressure at work. Chances are very good that later on you found out that several of the other kids in the class didn't grasp the concept either. So why didn't they raise their hands? Peer pressure. Peer pressure can very often lead to a situation where everyone *wants* to do the same thing, but everybody is *afraid* to do it because of what the others might think.

The question that arises out of all of this is: How can we as parents help our children stand up for their beliefs?

ENCOURAGE THAT SPECIAL FRIENDSHIP

I believe that one of the best things we as parents can do is to reinforce and encourage that one special friendship our son or daughter might have. With a little help from you in nurturing that relationship, your teenager will discover a special bond between himself and a friend, someone who will support him when he is faced with a decision that might go against the peer group's standards.

For example, you can encourage your son or daughter to bring a friend along on a family weekend. This will go a long way in strengthening the relationship between the adolescent and his friend, and it will also give the family the experience of doing some things together.

A word of caution is in order, though, when it comes to friends. You simply cannot pick your children's friends for them. Saying something like, "Mary, why don't you invite that little Thompson girl over to spend the night?" is apt to be resented, or to be greeted with a response such as, "Kathy Thompson? Mom, you've got to be kidding. I can't stand her!"

If you think the Thompsons' daughter is a very nice girl, and you'd like your own daughter to become friends with her, you might invite the entire Thompson family over for dinner. If you do that, there is at least a chance that the girls will hit it off, and you're not going to look like a "pushy" parent who's trying to run your daughter's life.

It can also be a good idea to talk to your children about their friends, finding out who they like, who they don't like, and why. It's been my experience that we parents are not always the best judge of an adolescent's character. We are quite susceptible to a snow job on the part of an Eddie Haskell-like character, so listen to what your kids have to say about the other members of their peer group. The last thing you want to do is encourage your son or daughter to become close friends with the wrong person.

BE MORE OBVIOUS IN YOUR INFLUENCE

How many hours a day do you spend with your children? Two? One? Sometimes only a few minutes a day?

In this hectic world it's easy for parents and kids to be isolated from one another. And when we might have time on weekends to spend with our kids, it's often true that our activity-conscious society fills our schedules to such an extent that no time is left for the family.

We talk a great deal about the "quality" time we give our kids as opposed to quantity time. But, really, all your kids understand is "time." They just need to be with you, to observe your life day in and day out. Of course, this puts a great burden on parents to monitor their own lives.

I believe it is the wise parent who tells his kids what he believes and why he believes it. But, above all, it's wiser to *show* them what he believes by the way he lives his life. It does very little good for a parent to lecture his children on the evils of smoking while he's lighting up a cigarette—or for him to tell his kids that they must say no to drugs while he's mixing himself a whiskey sour.

When I think of the influence we all have on our kids' lives I think of a woman I'll call Sally. Sally had a 17-year-old daughter named Sarah. Sarah was a popular girl in her school—a member of the pom-pom squad and an attendant in the queen's court at the homecoming celebration. She was a beautiful girl with a sparkling personality, and she didn't lack for dates. Oh, yes . . . she was also an excellent student.

One day Sally answered the door to find Sarah's 17-year-old boyfriend standing there. He asked if he could come in, and she said, "Sure, Bob . . . come on in." Naturally, she was curious as to why the young man had decided to pay her a visit, but she wasn't prepared for his comment: "Mrs. J., what is it with Sarah? How come I'm not getting any?"

Let me say right here that if anyone ever had the audacity to say something like that to me about one of my daughters he most likely wouldn't live long enough to hear the answer. All of my training in psychology would go right out the window, along with the fellow who asked the question.

Sally, however, handled the situation much better than I would have. To say she was shocked would be an understatement, but she managed to pull herself together, look Bob in the eye, and say, "You and I have to talk." (As hard as this might seem to believe, this conversation actually took place.)

Sarah's mom went right after Bob. She started out, "When I was seventeen I hated sauerkraut, despised it. I couldn't stand the smell of it. It made me want to vomit just to think about it. Today I'm forty-one years old and I love sauerkraut. There's not a thing I love more in the world than sauerkraut.

"Now as you know, my daughter and I have a good relationship. We talk about a lot of things. In fact, I know that my daughter is thinking about breaking up with you tonight. The reason is that she is sick and tired of your constant harassing her for sex. I think, Bob, that what my daughter's trying to tell you is that she's not ready for sex. And we hope that when the day comes that she is ready, she will be married.

"I know that's how she feels right now. She's telling you plainly and clearly that she doesn't like sauerkraut and she wants no part of it in her life now. And because of your immature attitude toward her feelings she's ready to quit seeing you."

You can bet those words took Bob back a few paces.

Sarah didn't stop seeing the boy right away. And on another occasion, as conversation developed around the same topic, he told Sarah's mom that he felt all kinds of pressure from the other guys in his peer group. After every date with Sarah, when he saw the guys at school the following morning, they'd start razzing him, wanting to know how far he'd gotten.

And to questions like, "Hey, Bob . . . you get any last night?" he was unable to respond with something like, "Knock it off. I really care about the girl."

Peer pressure prevented any such admission.

The interesting thing is that with the insight given by this wise mother, Bob was able to back off, in spite of the peer pressure he was facing. When he got it straight in his head that Sarah didn't want any part of premarital sex, their relationship turned around completely. He took the pressure off Sarah and the two of them became *more intimate,* in the truest sense of the word. They could enjoy each other's company and simply have fun together without the pressures of whether and when they were going to become sexually involved. They truly liked each other, especially when the hassles and strains were removed from their relationship.

Now just think about how good the relationship had to be

between Sally and Sarah. If I had the authority or the opportunity to give a mother-of-the year award, this mother would certainly be a top candidate—a mother who resisted the temptation to tear out this young man's spleen and, instead, sat down and gave him some good and wise counsel.

How good it would be if every parent could really talk about everything with his or her adolescent. We as parents get very few shots at them as they're growing up, and believe me when I tell you that they grow up very, very quickly. We don't seem to have enough time along the way to express to them what's really important in our lives. But when we dig down deep and share out of our own personal experiences and feelings, that's when we really give our children carte blanche to discuss with us anything that's on their minds. Such a relationship doesn't come naturally. It takes a great deal of hard work, including a willingness to listen and a demonstration of mutual respect and love between parent and child, to get to that point.

Always remember, your teenager needs to have your positive influence in his life.

SELECT THE ENVIRONMENT

How much time does your child spend in school? Perhaps six or seven hours a day? That's a pretty good chunk of his time.

Have you thought about *where* you want your children to go to school?

It's no secret that private and parochial school enrollments are surging. And one reason for that is that many parents believe the public school system does a beautiful job of teaching kids to be irresponsible; that there is little discipline, closeness, or warmth between teacher and child, and too many things going on there that are negative influences on our children.

I'm not suggesting that you should send your child to a private school. The decision as to whether or not to do that is entirely up to you. But if you *are* going to do it you had better make the decision early, instead of waiting until the fourth or fifth grade when he's going to say, "No, I don't want to go. I don't want to leave my friends." If you want your child in a private school, it's best to have him start his schooling there, in order to maximize the influence of the school's environment.

If you do have children who are young enough to be placed in a private school, the choice sounds easy at this point, doesn't it? All you have to do is pick the closest private school for your children or else go the public school route. But it's not really that easy. Suppose you choose to send your child to a private school. You better take a long, hard look at the various private schools in your community before you pick one. Don't think that all private schools are the same, because they're not, or that a private school is necessarily going to be better than a public school, because it isn't.

I hope that you're interested enough to go down to the school while it's in session to see how things are done there —and take your son or daughter with you when you go.

School is one place where you want to be very sure your child is in a positive and healthful environment.

You can also see to it that your home life is a positive environment. If our adolescents are going to deal with a world that says, "Conform, be like everybody else," then our teenagers must see positive relationships within their families—relationships that seem to say that someone really does care about them.

They need to know now, more than ever, that Mom and Dad really do care about each other. And if the two of you haven't been getting along, then perhaps you ought to seek out some counseling, for the sake of your marriage as well as for the sake of your children.

HELP THEM ADJUST TO CHANGE

They say that there are only two things certain in this world: death and taxes. I'd like to add a third thing to that short list, though, and that is change. Change is constant and it is unstoppable. Everything changes. People change, relationships change, situations change, environments change. You name it, and chances are very good that it changes.

I remember the "Peanuts" cartoon a few years back in which several of the characters are sitting out in the yard at night, looking up at the stars. They're talking about how the stars are permanent fixtures in the sky, and what great comfort can be derived from that—and the next thing you know, a shooting star streaks across the sky—completely destroying all of the talk about permanence and comfort.

Well, change is stressful for everyone, but particularly for adolescents. Parents have to help their teenagers cope with change; yet, many times the parents are also trying to adjust to the same changes.

Richard came to me a few years ago because he was in trouble with the law. He was only 17, but he had just taken part in an armed robbery. He had also admitted to taking part in at least 16 burglaries. You know, just your average all-

American kid who was looking at a lengthy stay in juvenile hall—or maybe even in the state pen, since there was some talk of trying him as an adult.

Richard was the oldest child in his family, and at the time Richard came for therapy his mother was seeking the dissolution of her marriage of 22 years. Now I'm not going to say that if Richard's parents hadn't been going through a divorce, he never would have wound up in trouble. I'm not going to say it—but I'm tempted to. And I'm tempted to because it became obvious during therapy that the most powerful feelings he had inside of him centered around his parents' impending divorce.

I really believe that Richard felt that life was being unfair to him and that, basically, it had kicked him squarely in the teeth. He was striking back in any and every way he could think of.

Not only was Richard going through a change because of his parents' divorce, but the family had just moved from the Boston area to the Southwest. Breaking into a new peer group is a very difficult assignment for some kids, and this was definitely the case with Richard. He had to become acquainted with what his peers in this new setting expected of him; he had to reestablish himself in an entirely new environment. Although he was an athlete, he had moved in the fall and his sport wasn't played until spring, so he couldn't use baseball as a way of initiating friendships. So Richard felt very isolated and lonely. These two changes in his life really laid the foundation for peer pressure. The need to conform made Richard, who had always been a pretty good kid, become involved in some things that were not characteristic of his prior life.

One of the other guys who had been involved in the armed robbery had been sitting next to Richard in a class at school and had introduced himself. Richard's first thought was "At last! A friend!" It may not have been the friend Richard would have picked if he had been able to sit back and choose the friends he wanted, but it was somebody—and at this point he was looking for just about *anybody* to reach out to him.

So here's this kid, who's never really been a discipline problem—and all of a sudden he finds himself driving the getaway car for an armed robbery, as well as being involved in 16 burglaries.

I know that the time we spent talking about his feelings was very good for Richard. But, unfortunately, there was nothing I could do to rearrange what had already taken place, and Richard wound up serving time for the crimes he had committed.

What is the best way to help your child adjust to changes in his life? Simply to talk to him about them.

Let him know that you understand how he feels. Give him reassurances that he will soon feel better. When you do, he may respond by saying something like, "No I won't! I'll be miserable for the rest of my life!" Try not to jump all over him for saying something like that. Almost all adolescents are prone to exaggeration and hyperbole, but he heard what you said and he will draw comfort from it, whether he wants to admit it or not.

When your child is going through a period of change, he needs for you to allow him the freedom to vent his feelings. He also needs you to stay especially close to him. This is a good time for trips to the ballgame, the amusement park, etc.

And again, if the changes are simply too much for him to handle, it can be an excellent idea to seek out professional counseling.

HELP THEM SAY NO

Another thing you can do for your adolescents is to help them say no.

And here's a news flash for you. Sometimes your kids ask you if they can do something or go somewhere, and they're hoping that you're going to say no to it.

One mother told me that she was really angry when her teenage daughter called from one of her friend's houses and asked if she could do something or other—I don't remember what it was, but it was something that the girl should have known Mom was going to say no to. And that's exactly what Mom did, in a not-too-nice way: "Of course you can't do that! How could you even ask me! You ought to know better!" And on and on.

Later on, when her daughter got home she said, "I didn't mean to make you mad, Mom. I knew you'd say no. In fact, I *wanted* you to say no. But they wouldn't quit bugging me about it until I called and asked you."

You see, it's easier for a kid to say, "My mean old mom won't let me," than it is to say, "I don't want to." And I think it's perfectly fine to let your kid off the hook by being the bad ol' meanie when a bad ol' meanie is called for.

Perhaps it hasn't happened to you yet, but sooner or later your teenager will be talking to one of his or her friends on the phone and say, "Oh . . . I don't know . . . let me ask my mom (or dad)."

Then, he'll call out to you, loud enough for the person on the other end of the line to hear, "Hey, mom . . . can I . . ." whatever it is his friends are asking him to do. But even as he's asking you, he's shaking his head no.

What he's looking for is an easy way to get out of doing something he doesn't really want to do. The wise parent will say, "No . . . I don't want you doing that sort of thing," and she'll say it loudly enough to be heard by the person on the other end of the line.

Always remember that it's hard to say no . . . especially when you're a teenager facing all of the pressures of the peer group.

When I was a little boy, my friend Moonhead and I would walk along the village roads in the summertime, anxiously watching for a driver to flip a cigarette butt out of a window of a passing car. We'd run to get the butt that we didn't even need matches for. I'm sure we smoked for lots of reasons— to seem like big boys, to impress our peers, to feel more grown up, to look older than we were, etc. The first time I ever smoked a cigarette I was seven years old, and I continued smoking until I got smart and quit when I was 22. (That was about the same time I met my wife—in the men's room of a local hospital. But that's a long story we don't have time to get into—yet.)

As a teenager, I really didn't know how harmful cigarettes could be. There was some talk about how destructive smoking was, but not nearly as much as today. Now it's even spelled out on the package: "Surgeon General's Warning: Smoking Causes Lung Cancer, Heart Disease, Emphysema, and May Complicate Pregnancy." Yet even though it's right there on the carton, millions of people still smoke. My point is that although we know things aren't good for us, we continue to do them.

Now when do most people start smoking? Does a 40-year-old walk into the store one day and say, "I'd like a pack of cigarettes, please. I think I'm going to learn how to smoke."

No, the average cigarette smoker starts in his teens—or earlier, like I did—and he does it for two reasons: (1) the other kids are doing it, and (2) it's a way to look cool. The sad thing is that by the time he knows better, he's hooked. If only he could have said no to smoking in the first place.

It's not always easy to do the things we know we should do. For example, which day of the week do you suppose is the most popular day to start a diet? Mondays? You're right. Why Mondays? Because Monday, being the first day of the working week, makes it easier on Saturday night to lie to ourselves as we reach for that second piece of pie. We tell ourselves, "I can have this pie now because, after all, I'm going on a diet on Monday." Even though we know that all that sugar isn't good for us, and even though we know we shouldn't use tobacco, we adults have a terrible time saying no.

And if that's how it is with us, just imagine how hard it is for an adolescent, with peer pressure as strong as it is, to say no to one hit on a marijuana cigarette or one snort of cocaine. My experience with teenagers tells me that they consciously know that many of the things they do are not good for them, and that left to their own devices they would never do them, but they don't have the self-esteem or self-control to say no when their peers are saying, "Come on . . . try it!"

Parents must help their children develop self-discipline, which leads to a good self-image. When your adolescent feels good about himself, he is going to have a much easier time during this period of his life.

I have seen low self-esteem lead a child into various types of tragedy—involvement in crime, drug abuse, promiscuity —and even suicide.

We all know that over the past 20 to 25 years, American teenagers have been killing themselves in ever increasing numbers. Every day in our country 13 teenagers take their own lives. Even though, as I write this, the teen suicide rate has gone down slightly over the past few months, it's still alarmingly high, and I'm sure you agree with me that one teenage suicide a year is way too many.

How tragic it is that a young person who has his whole life ahead of him should decide, "I don't have anything to live for," or "I'm never going to be any good," and take his life.

Why do they do it?

Sometimes it's because their parents have never learned how to discipline them without abusing them, saying things like, "You're so stupid . . . you'll never amount to anything," and "Sometimes I wish you'd never been born," and assorted other little gems that can crush the spirit and soul right out of a teenager.

Sometimes it's because the momentary pressures of life get blown all out of proportion. The child believes there is no way out of his present dilemma except to put an end to his existence—but the truth is that if he will only hang on and work through it, the problem will be resolved within a couple of weeks. Teenagers get depressed because of the breakup of a romantic relationship, because they feel they've let their parents down, because nobody loves them, because they're afraid of leaving childhood behind and moving on into adulthood, etc. There are many reasons why children kill themselves, but ultimately all of these reasons can be traced back to low self-esteem.

By my own observation I've seen that many teenagers who have taken their own lives were actually extremely good students in school and were highly thought of by others.

However, the important thing to remember is how they saw themselves. Maybe they grew up in an environment where Dad pushed the level of expectation so high that the teenager was defeated by the overly high demands placed upon him. Or to get Mom and Dad off the hook, perhaps the child placed these high expectations on himself. I haven't seen any suicide statistics among firstborn children or only children, but I wouldn't be surprised to find that there was an extremely high incidence of suicide among these children because of their perfectionistic natures.

Several years ago, Patrick McHenry, Carl Tishler, and Karen Christman wrote an article titled, "Adolescent Suicide and the Classroom Teacher," which was published in *The Education Digest*. Even though the information is several years old, it still applies and is worth repeating here.[1]

The authors studied the behavior of dozens of adolescents who had committed or attempted suicide, and in the majority of those cases they found that the adolescent had exhibited the following changes in behavior prior to trying to take his life:

1. A drastic change in personal appearance from good to bad.

2. Somatic complaints—constant stomachaches, backaches, headaches, diarrhea, etc.

3. An inability to concentrate.

4. Dramatic shifts in the quality of their schoolwork.

5. Changes in daily behavioral patterns which could manifest themselves in extreme fatigue, excessive sleeping, withdrawal, decreased appetite, emotional outbursts, use of alcohol and drugs, loss of friends, and an overwhelming sense of guilt and shame.

The investigators also cited crises which are accompanied by the aforementioned behavioral changes: the death of a family member, relative, or close friend; separation of parents, siblings, or relatives; personal problems with the law or someone close having problems with the law; plus others.

The writers suggest that discussing suicide will not make the depressed adolescent more inclined to commit suicide; rather, he is emotionally relieved by the opportunity to discuss his feelings.

I know it is downright scary to even think about teenage suicide. But I really believe we could prevent such tragedies in our teenagers' lives if we would dedicate ourselves to honest communication with them. That is, when we get brave enough to share some of *our* thoughts and feelings with our children, it gives *them* permission to discuss theirs with us.

Remember, prior to the teen years, plant the seed in your adolescent's mind that the coming years may be stormy ones. Then when the time comes that your son or daughter begins to experience some weird, crazy, upsetting feelings, and finds himself tempted to withdraw and keep everything inside, he'll know at least that what he's experiencing isn't unique. He won't think there's something wrong with him for feeling this way—and he'll know that even his parents had similar feelings and experiences—and that they survived them.

That seed you planted years earlier will germinate and grow within him and, hopefully, give him the strength to ward off some of those feelings of desolation and loneliness he may be experiencing. Then the door will once again be open for you and your teenager to discuss the problems and emotions he is facing. And if he doesn't have to face them alone, he has a much better chance of surviving his teen years intact.

TAKE ACTION

• There are several board games which can be used as a springboard to talking about choices that must be faced by adolescents, and parents too, on a daily basis. In this age of electronic gadgetry, board games can still be great fun, and they can open up communication between kids and parents. For example, the version of the game *Scruples* which is designed specifically for adolescents, presents several hypothetical situations and then asks the players to tell how they would respond to those situations. It's not my intention to recommend that particular game—but there are other such games that can help you better understand what your kids are thinking about the issues they face every day.

• Plan a family outing and allow each of your children to bring along one special friend. It doesn't have to be anything fancy—a night of miniature golf or bowling, a picnic at the beach, mountains, or local park, a trip to the skating rink, a visit to the ballpark. The idea is to encourage the development of those special friendships that can be so important to adolescents.

• Take the time to write a letter to your adolescent, telling him how much you appreciate him. You can let him know that you're proud that he's your kid, that you know you don't let him know often enough how you feel about him, even tell him that you're sorry if you seem to be on his back all the time. Your 14-year-old may seem embarrassed if you tell him you love him, but he still needs to hear it, and if you say it in a letter, it will probably become one of his most treasured possessions.

1. Patrick C. McHenry, Carl L. Tishler, and Karen L. Christman, "Adolescent Suicide and the Classroom Teacher," *The Education Digest* (September 1980), pp. 43–45.

3

The Dating Game

Drive past any high school just before or after school lets out, and you're probably going to be embarrassed.

Why? Because you're going to see a few young men and women who seem to be joined at the lips. Actually, you're liable to see the same thing if you drive past a junior high school, because kids today are getting involved with the opposite sex earlier than ever before. And that's easy to understand when you see how movies and television, along with books and magazines, are always pushing sex in their faces.

Yes, yes, I admit that back in my day boys and girls were making out. But they were doing it in cars on back country roads, out of everyone else's view, or on a front porch in the dark. They weren't doing it right on the school steps as hundreds of other kids walked past them on their way into or out of school. Not only are kids today getting interested in the opposite sex earlier, but they're flaunting it as never before.

The fact is that adolescent boys are generally crazy about adolescent girls, and adolescent girls feel the same way about adolescent boys. I've heard it said that love makes the world go round and that there's nothing like young love, and I suppose that's true. But young love can also be a very difficult situation if kids haven't been taught how to control themselves, and if they don't really know what love and sex are all about.

Since time began, boys and girls have been drawn to each other like bees to honey. However, in many traditional cultures dating was never an option because the parents chose their children's future mates. But in our society dating is a very appropriate way to get to know which qualities you are looking for in a lifetime mate.

Now I admit that I've had teenagers tell me, "Nobody dates anymore." They just meet at parties, or go to the movies together, or what have you.

But don't you believe it for a minute. They may not refer to it as dating—and much of it may not be the traditional standard of "dinner and a movie"—but they're still dating, and the old rules still ought to apply.

Now I believe that teenagers should be intimate in their dating—but not physically intimate. As a young man begins to date one young woman more than any others, his goal should be to discover as many things about her as he can. And her goal should be to discover as many things about him as she can. How does she think about certain things? Can he share some of his own burdens and hurts with her? Can he take off his mask and let her see the real him without getting that feeling of rejection?

Why should kids date, anyway? Is it really important?

Yes, I think it is important. It's a maturing experience which ought to sharpen communication skills and bring about growth in other necessary social graces. And I believe that there is a bigger danger in marrying the first boy or girl who comes along than there is in dating many other people.

65

There is something to be said for "comparison shopping." But as important as dating is, there are several factors that have to be considered with regard to it.

DON'T PUSH YOUR KIDS INTO DATING

From what I've discovered through my work with families, many kids start dating because their parents have pushed them into it, sometimes at a very early age.

Mom thinks it's "cute" to help her 11-year-old daughter get dressed up so she can go to the Saturday afternoon matinee with her boyfriend. Dad wants his 12-year-old son to be a chip off the old block, so he pushes him to ask the girl across the street for a date. Dad will be happy to be the chauffeur.

Have you ever heard an adult say to a child who's only six or seven years old, "Got a girlfriend (or boyfriend) yet?"

Now what does this convey to the youngster? "Gee, I guess I'm a loser if I don't have a girlfriend. I'd better start looking for one."

It's unfortunate that kids are being forced to grow up early like this. My advice is to let them play with toys and games as long as they can—they'll discover the opposite sex soon enough, and that will happen without any prodding from Mom and Dad.

Too much too quickly seems to be in vogue in modern-day America. Parents and peers literally force the young boy or girl to concentrate on "boyfriend" or "girlfriend" rather than just "friends." Kids need to spend several years developing friendships with members of both sexes.

It's not only the parents who push their children into early dating. Other kids at school can be cruel, and it has become commonplace for a young child who doesn't have a "special friend" of the opposite sex to be taunted and asked if he is gay. I knew of one perfectly normal 10-year-old boy who was being called "fag" by the older boys in his neighborhood (boys who were 12 and 13) simply because he did not have a girlfriend. I realize that children have always teased each other, and that name-calling should be ignored. But it's one thing to be called "ape-brain" or "four-eyes," or some of the other favored names of days gone by, and quite another thing to be called "fag" or "queer." When someone calls you something like that, and does it in an extremely derogatory tone of voice, the only thing you can do is set out to prove that the name doesn't fit.

Teens and even preteens often begin dating because of peer pressure. And as we've talked about before, what kids their own age feel and think during these turbulent years usually far outweighs what Mom and Dad think. So even if you never encouraged dating as your kids were growing up, by the time they are in junior high school, peer pressure is probably going to make it very important to them.

THERE IS A NEED TO BE NOTICED

If you've ever taken your adolescent out shopping for clothes, you've undoubtedly seen firsthand that status is very important to him.

He can have these pants which are $15, or these pants which are $45. The $45 pants look just like the $15 pants, with the exception of that brand name on the hip pocket. The $15 pants might even be a little bit better so far as quality is concerned.

But no, they won't do. Your child has to have the more

expensive pair. And all because that name on the hip pocket says, "These pants are cool, and so is the kid who's wearing them."

That need for status reaches into just about every other area of the adolescent's life. He not only feels a need to wear the right clothes, and do the right things, but to be seen with the right people. There may be little or no emotional feeling for the person he's dating, just a desire to be seen with someone else who is considered cool by the rest of his peers. The someone he dates—or would like to—thus has to look "good"—have a neat hairstyle, a good physical appearance—and "be cool." But unless he meets those standards himself, he won't find anyone to date him. And this is where many young people meet head-on with an identity crisis.

I remember one young man who was despondent because he could not find a date. He was an average boy, a 16-year-old junior in high school, fairly good-looking, and he should have been able to get a date without any real trouble.

But he couldn't do it. On closer inspection of the problem, though, it turned out that first of all, most of the girls he was interested in were older than he. The current object of his desire was an 18-year-old senior who had just been elected homecoming queen. It was hard to get her to notice him, especially because her current boyfriend was a 21-year-old college sophomore. Prior to the homecoming queen, he had tried to get a date with the pretty girl who also happened to be president of the student body. She had politely turned him down.

Perhaps his was an extreme case, and he was certainly setting his sights exceptionally high—but that's typical of attitudes to be found among adolescents.

Now everybody at any age wants to be noticed. Nobody wants to be neutral, invisible, a nonperson. But the desire to have people notice you can almost be an obsession during the adolescent years.

When I was a college sophomore I got myself into some hot water with school officials. What happened was that one evening the ice cream machine in the dorm where I lived went on the blink and began to give away freebies. All of the guys who lived in the dorm proceeded to go down to the lobby and rip off the machine. Of course, the dorm lost quite a bit of money during the course of the evening, with the result that a couple of days later the head resident put up a sign which said, "All of you who participated in the unauthorized ice cream social the other evening, please put your money in this box." His sign went on to explain how much money the dorm had lost, and there was a cardboard box where we could all put in enough money to make up for the ice cream we had taken.

My roommate and I came in, saw the sign sitting next to the switchboard, and also saw that the old gentleman who sat at the switchboard was sound asleep. We looked at each other and knew, without saying a thing, that the same thought was going through both our minds: *Wouldn't it be funny if we ripped off the conscience fund?*

So that's what we did. We took all the money out of that box, and like most 19-year-olds who do something to be noticed, we had to tell the whole world. We told the world by throwing a party for the guys in our wing, and it didn't take long for word to get down to the head resident and to the dean of students, that Kevin Leman and his roommate were responsible for stealing the dorm's money.

We had wanted to be noticed and we were. We were kicked out of school—which was a lot more notice than we had bargained for.

Teenagers have a sometimes desperate need to be noticed. They will go to great lengths to get the attention of the peer group, and especially those members of the peer group who belong to the opposite sex. They reason, "How will I get dates if nobody sees me?"

In the first chapter, I talked about the importance of communicating with your children about sex, and recommended that mothers talk to their sons and fathers to their daughters about this most important subject.

And when you do, there are two important truths you need to get across: First of all, your adolescent needs to know that people are people whether they are male or female, and all human beings are deserving of honor and respect. Your children may not immediately begin acting in accordance with what you've said, but they need to hear you tell them that people are not to be used for any reason, and that includes enhancing your own status.

The second thing you need to tell them is that you cannot judge a person on the basis of his or her physical appearance. It may be a cliché to say that a beautiful face can hide an evil heart, but it's absolutely true. Tell your children that if they limit themselves to "beautiful" and "cool" people, then they are cutting themselves off from getting to know some people who may be intelligent, fun, interesting, and very pleasant company.

Let me tell you, I've known some beautiful women who were—to be absolutely frank—excruciatingly boring. They were self-centered and could rattle on for what seemed like hours about things that only they were interested in. Would I put all "beautiful women" into this category? Of course not. I happen to be married to a beautiful woman who is also intelligent, interesting, giving—a wonderful person. But my point is that it is true when they tell you that a book can't be judged by its cover.

70

Again, your words of wisdom may not immediately change your adolescent's behavior. He may still spend all his time chasing after those who can give him status—but it will benefit him, if not now then later, to hear your words of wisdom on this subject.

A friend of mine told me he will always be haunted by an incident that occurred when he was in high school. It seems there was one girl in his class who was the brunt of many jokes, simply because she had a harelip. Some of the kids thought she was retarded, because she *looked* different.

The truth was that she was a better than average student, but she didn't have any friends because no one would give her a chance.

Well, halfway through the semester, my friend dropped a math class and added a study hall to his schedule. Much to his chagrin, he found himself assigned to a desk right next to Rachel, the girl with the harelip.

He didn't say anything to her at first, but eventually because he was bored, he started talking to her. And once he got past the obvious impediment, he discovered that she was a bright and fun person. He really enjoyed sitting next to her.

But one day in the school cafeteria, he was sitting with some friends of his who started talking about some of the tough luck they were having in one of their classes. And for no reason other than the fact that he wanted to say something clever, my friend said, "Oh, yeah. Well, you guys don't have half the trouble I've got in study hall. Guess who I've got sitting next to me? . . . Rachel . . . that's who! Yuck!!!"

No sooner had the words left his mouth than he looked behind him and saw Rachel sitting at the next table. She was looking down at her lunch, pretending that she hadn't heard, but it was obvious that she had.

My friend remembers that he wanted to apologize to her, but he didn't have the courage. He went the rest of the year without saying more than a few words to her. Several times he planned to apologize, but every time he saw her he was so ashamed of himself that he just couldn't do it.

"I really liked her," he told me. "I would have liked to have taken her out . . . or at least I would have liked to be her friend, to let the other kids know she was really pretty cool.

"But instead, I feel like I knifed her in the back."

He says he hasn't seen Rachel for nearly 15 years now. He doesn't know where she is or what she's doing. Chances are that she's long ago forgotten that incident in the school cafeteria, but my friend will never forget.

What's the point of this story? Simply that your children need to hear you tell them that physical beauty and status are not nearly as important as what's inside a person. Beauty is not always obvious at first glance. It's true, too, that a good person actually becomes better looking the more you know him!

NECESSITY—THE MOTHER OF INVENTION

I had always been rather curious about the dating habits of college students, so while I was at the University of Arizona campus I did a survey to determine just how many students who lived in the dormitories dated at least once a week. I discovered that a surprisingly low 15 percent of these college students dated on a regular basis. One might think that on a college campus of 35,000 students there would be all kinds of opportunities to date. But although they walked by thousands of members of the opposite sex every day, there was very little of males and females getting to know each other on a one-to-one basis.

Picture what was going on on a Saturday night. All the guys were sitting around their dorm going, "Oh, man, it's so boring. Here we are sitting around doing nothing, and all the girls are out having a good time."

And over at the girls' dorm, all the ladies were sitting around saying, "It's so boring here. All we do is sit around and watch television and all the guys are out having a good time."

They would have had a great time if they could have gotten together, but nobody would take the initiative.

Well, necessity is the mother of invention, and what this means with regard to dating is that if you're lonely and looking for a date, it doesn't do a bit of good to sit around waiting for the phone to ring.

Now because I personally think that by the time an adolescent reaches college age he should be dating, I encouraged the students I worked with to meet people. I'll never forget what happened when four young coeds who had heard me speak at freshman orientation took me up on my invitation to come visit me in my office if I could be of any service. They were all a little apprehensive and had trouble getting to the reason for their visit. But finally, one young woman who seemed to be the spokesperson for the group said they were disappointed because they hadn't met any men on the campus, and they wondered if I might have any suggestions for them.

I explained to them that there was a big difference between high school and college, and now they would have to take things into their own hands and create the environment that would attract the type of guys they were looking for. I asked them if they would be willing to do something a little bit crazy. They looked at each other inquisitively and gave a unanimous halfhearted shrug of their shoulders, which I took to mean that they were willing. I suggested that they take a popcorn popper to one of our largest men's residence halls, go into the lobby, sit down, and begin popping corn.

Well, just as I had advertised, it sounded a little crazy, but to their credit they were willing to take a chance. So they walked into Santa Cruz Hall armed with a popper, oil, butter, popcorn, some bowls, and a sheet to spread out on the floor. They told me later that they kept looking at each other as if to say, "I can't believe we're actually doing this. I feel so stupid." But there were four of them, and because there is strength in numbers, they kept moving forward.

They spread out the sheet, plugged in the popcorn popper, and began to pop corn. As the aroma worked its way up the stairwell of the men's residence hall, about 40 guys, like bears awakening from a long winter's nap, lumbered toward the lobby area. Forty to four—those aren't bad odds for anyone!

As it turned out, the girls had a great time. They wanted to meet guys, and that's exactly what they did. By the end of the evening, the four of them had paired off with four guys, and they all went out together for pizza. I suppose it was dessert after all that popcorn.

The following evening these four guys decided to have a popcorn party of their own in the lobby of the women's dormitory, and it, too, was a hot-buttered success.

So when dating begins to get critical, your teenagers may have to take matters into their own hands and create situations where they can meet others. But they must be sure the situation is going to draw the kind of guys or girls they want to meet. Remind them that those who go to singles bars to meet people are likely to meet people who like to hang around in bars.

Your daughter says she doesn't know any boys? Is she active in some school clubs? Does she go to school events—football games, basketball games, plays, dances, etc.?

If you want to meet interesting people, you have to go where such people congregate. And if you don't know of any such events, you may have to do what the girls at the University of Arizona did, and create an event of your own!

BEING NOTICED FOR THE RIGHT REASONS

I can think of one young woman I recently counseled who tried to get men to notice her by hitchhiking. She got three men to notice her, all right, but not in the way she wanted. They picked her up, took her out into the desert where they beat her, robbed her of her money, forced her to perform several sex acts with them, and then left her, bloodied and naked. She is fortunate that they didn't kill her, but she will be a long time getting over what they did do to her.

Teenagers want to be noticed, to be special and above average. Yet, by their very nature they see themselves as awkward, gawky, uncoordinated, and klutzy. Although your teenager may see himself that way, you must let him know that that's not at all how you see him, that you think he's a very special person. You can help see to it that a positive self-concept takes root.

It's important for a child to learn that he is good and capable, and that his mother, father, brothers, and sisters care for him. If we are able to create an environment within the home where a kid can grow and learn about himself and others without a constant fear of rejection or ridicule, then that growth can be quite positive.

So many times I see parents become tremendous flaw-pickers, pointing out all the shortcomings and faults of their teenagers. This sort of discouraging experience during the turbulent adolescent years can do nothing but drive the kid from home and get him hooked into whatever's in vogue in the peer group.

In his book *Teaching Your Child to Make Decisions,* Gordon Porter Miller gives several suggestions for parents who want to be supportive of their teenagers, and I believe these are particularly applicable to the dating experience. They are:

- Always show love and support, even in the most difficult situations.
- Clarify and stick to limits and consequences.
- Take your child's problems (and fears) seriously.
- Keep things in perspective.

He also says that teenagers may represent a living paradox to their parents because they may be both:

- Impulsive and thoughtful
- Shy and confident
- Rude and sensitive
- Daring and cautious
- Individualistic and conforming
- Arrogant and timid
- Tough and scared
- Omnipotent-feeling and powerless
- Mature and childish.[1]

He's absolutely right about all of these things, and I'm sure you can see how each of these personality traits can impact upon a teenager's dating experiences. For example, one moment a teenage boy will be terrified of girls, and the next minute he'll see himself as a lady-killer. He may seem to be mature in his relationships with girls one minute, and then spend several hours moping in his room because he tried to call a special girl who isn't home—and he's just *sure* she doesn't like him anymore. (Somehow, he thinks that her appreciation of him is tied to her waiting at home for his phone call.) That's the way it is with teenagers!

Now, people often ask me why so many of my examples come from very young children. That's because the training of a child really occurs in the first seven years of his life. If we make the right choices then, things will be much easier for us later on.

When it comes to teenagers, the truth is that they can pretty much do whatever they want to in life. It's only out of respect and love that they allow their parents to parent them at all. The teenager who really wants to be rebellious— who wants to give his parents the hassle of their lifetime — certainly has the ability to do so.

SETTING THE GUIDELINES

Okay, you probably have a 16- or 17-year-old son or daughter and you're thinking, "Thanks a lot, Leman. What am I supposed to do—go back in a time machine so my child will be small again, and I can make the right decisions this time around?"

Of course not. But one of the things you can do at this stage, if you haven't been a responsible parent in the past—

if you haven't disciplined your kids and haven't tried to put things into a proper perspective—is to start off with an apology. Say, "I'm sorry for what I've done in the past, but things are going to be different from now on." It's true that if you're having problems now, you'd be much better off if you'd made the proper decisions in the past, but it's *never* too late to start doing things right.

Now, let's get down to talk about dating regulations. What are some of the guidelines?

Of course, every individual is different, but I think 16 is a good age for an adolescent to begin dating one-on-one. I think that in group situations, kids can certainly be dating as early as 14 or 15, as long as they understand that dating is permissible at that early age only in groups.

There is a tremendous danger in letting teenagers begin dating too early. I had a 15-year-old girl tell me once that she was bored to tears by dating. She had started so young that she kept progressing further and further in order to keep the dating experience exciting. Now she was so sick of getting drunk, stoned, smashed, and making out that she'd had it. She wanted time out from guys, because she felt that she had already been raked over the coals too many times. And you know what? She was right. She had not even reached her "sweet sixteenth" birthday, and she was already a jaded, cynical woman, and the hardness shone in her eyes.

Dating, regardless of all the social problems of the peer group, should be a time of having fun, of sharing time with somebody else, and getting to know other people. And I believe that the teenager in your home who is about to start dating should be encouraged to prepare his or her own guidelines for the dating process. Most kids basically know the problems that go along with dating, and most of them really don't want to get themselves involved in a situation they can't handle.

For instance, I knew of a 16-year-old girl whose parents allowed her to set her own curfew, suggesting that midnight was a good time. Let me tell you, those parents were pleasantly surprised to find their daughter coming home from her dates at ten or eleven. This is not at all unusual when teenagers are trusted to set some of their own guidelines. So let them prepare a list of do's and don'ts. I think that's a healthier way to start than for Mom and Dad to issue an edict on how things are going to be. One thing we know about young people is that if they have any input into rules and regulations there's a higher probability that they will adhere to them. Of course, there will have to be some discussion between parents and kids concerning the list, and probably some give and take as well.

If your teenager's list includes staying out until four in the morning and going out every night of the week, then I certainly think some alterations are due. But I doubt if you'll find that's the sort of thing he does. Show him that you trust him, and chances are very good that he'll prove himself to be responsible.

Show him that you don't trust him, and he's just as apt to live up to your lack of trust.

Above all else, make sure that you keep those lines of communication open. And always bear in mind, communication is not a one-way street. I've known parents who *thought* they were communicating with their adolescents, when that wasn't the case at all. What they were doing was *preaching* and *lecturing,* but it was not *communicating.* Communication involves talking, and it also involves listening. It involves giving and it involves taking.

Tell your teenager how you feel. Share your innermost

feelings and secrets with him—but be sure to open up to him whenever he tries to tell you what's in his heart. This is especially true with regard to his blossoming interest in the opposite sex. If he tries to tell you something and you seem to be disinterested, he may decide that he'll never risk the hurt of trying to share himself with you again. If he tells you something that makes you recoil or react with shock, he'll decide that he can't afford to tell you what's really on his mind, but only what you *want* to hear.

The wise parent is one who remembers how it really was "way back then" when he was a teenager; who not only remembers how it was, in fact, but *admits* how it was—who doesn't try to gloss it over and pretend that he was perfect, and who doesn't try to convince himself that his relation-ships with the opposite sex were always as smooth as silk.

If you remember how it was, you're going to have a pretty good idea of some of the emotions and feelings your adoles-cent is experiencing, and you'll be able to help him through the most difficult of times. Yes, times change. It's not the same for kids today as it was for their parents. But even though times change, people really don't. Emotions are still the same. Feelings of awkwardness and inadequacy are still the same, and so are those feelings regarding the opposite sex—that strange mixture of curiosity, passion, and fear. Do you remember how you felt the first time you got up enough courage to ask Mary Lou for a date? Or the hours you spent waiting by the telephone hoping Johnny would call? If so, good . . . because those memories will definitely help you relate to your own teenager.

TAKE ACTION

• Play a "game" with your adolescent in which you ask him or her to list, in order of priority, the 10 most important things in a girlfriend or boyfriend. While he or she is preparing that list, draw up one of your own, guessing what your son or daughter is going to say. Once the two lists are finished compare them, seeing how many you got right and wrong, and use the occasion as a chance to talk about what's really important in a girlfriend or boyfriend and, thus, in a potential spouse.

• Take the time to sit down with your adolescent and draw up some "rules" with regard to dating. Allowing him to have input in the process, come up with some guidelines with regard to curfew, how often dating can take place, which activities are acceptable for dates and which are not, etc.

• If you have a child who is still several years away from adolescence, sit down with him or her and establish some rules for the future. Even if your little girl is only eight or nine years old, it's not too early to talk about what you will expect from her when those "dating days" get here. How old must she be before you'll let her go out on a one-to-one date with a boy? What will her curfew be when those days get here? And so on. By establishing guidelines now, you won't be in for any battles—or at least *as many* battles—when the child does begin dating.

• Get your spouse to join you in talking to your children about your first date. Was it great? Or was it a flop? Was it love at first sight, or did you think you'd never see each other again? Be gentle with each other, but be truthful with your kids. Dad, were you nervous when you went to pick her up? Mom, were you excited when he asked you out? Your kids will also benefit from your sharing of some of the "humorous" dating experiences you've had. They need to know that you remember what it was like, that you've "been there," and that you understand and support them in their ventures into the world of dating.

1. Gordon Porter Miller, *Teaching Your Child to Make Decisions* (New York: Harper & Row, 1984), p. 248.

4

A Fire Out of Control: Teens and Sex

Marianne's mother insisted that she and Kyle were spending too much time together.

But Marianne always reacted to her mother's expressed worries by saying, "What's the matter, Mom? Don't you trust me? I'm not going to let anything happen."

And she intended to live up to that promise. But one day they got to kissing a little bit too passionately. They were in Marianne's house, early afternoon, and her mother and father were both at work. They were all alone and could do anything they wanted to.

Before she knew what was happening, Kyle's hand was up her blouse and he was unsnapping her bra. She tried to tell him to stop, but she didn't want him to. And that's how Marianne lost her virginity.

Now she's afraid that she might be pregnant. Some of her friends had told her that it's impossible to get pregnant "the first time," but she's discovered, perhaps a bit too late, that that's not true.

I've seen this situation too many times to count. I've seen girls' lives all but destroyed when they find out that they're pregnant, and I've seen them cry tears of joy and swear that they'll behave themselves from now on, after they find out that it was only a false alarm.

For some of them, sex comes as the result of spending too much unchaperoned time with that "certain someone," and for others it comes as a determined effort to "go out and get laid." Teenage boys, especially, are obligated to "prove their manhood" by having sex as often as they can, but today just as many girls are anxious to leave their virginity behind.

The absolute truth is that insofar as unmarried teenagers are concerned, sex causes nothing but trouble—for girls and boys.

And it's a tragedy that so many young people try to make dating a purely sexual time together. They do this for several reasons, but the primary one, again, is peer pressure. The sex drive is there, certainly, but as strong as it may be, it's still secondary to the teenager's need to "prove himself" to the group. And then, too, the sex drive is like the appetite for food—it must be kept under control. Either the person controls the drive or the drive controls the person. If a teenager's appetite is out of control, he's going to put on 30 or 40 pounds or more—and that certainly won't be good for him. If his sexual appetite is out of control, that, too, can lead to physical and emotional problems.

I'm certain that if young men really knew how young women felt about sex they'd be shocked. You see, the most special physical act according to women is not sex, but just being held. Sometimes the boy who doesn't understand that thinks that he's expected to "perform," that his girlfriend is going to think he's a wimp if he doesn't at least try to get her into the sack. Let's face it, there's going to be some kind of physical touching between a young guy and girl as they go through the dating process. They're going to be holding hands, kissing, and touching in some way, shape, or form. Many of them are going to move on from there to petting, and from there, naturally, to intercourse. But that doesn't have to happen and, especially as far as teenagers are concerned, shouldn't happen. Males of all ages need to understand that women of all ages are the happiest when the men they love are showing them affection simply by holding them.

Several years ago I read an article in *Psychology Today* which talked about the fact that teenage girls and boys see things from quite different perspectives. A survey revealed that girls who wore hip-hugging jeans, short skirts, and tops without bras just thought they were being stylish. Boys, on the other hand, thought that such clothes advertised the girl's interest in sex. If she didn't want the guys to be after her, why was she so intent on showing them her body?

The survey also revealed that girls were more likely than boys to agree with the statement, "Sometimes I wish girls could just be friends with boys without worrying about sexual relationships."

If you are the parent of a teenage boy, you should teach your son that he does not have to "prove his manhood" through sexual conquest.

In his book *The Nine Most Troublesome Teenage Problems and How to Solve Them,* Dr. Lawrence Bauman writes that "compulsive Don Juan behavior is as much of a desperate attempt on the part of boys to build up self-esteem through an appeal to vulgar popularity as it can be a desperate attempt on the part of promiscuous girls to be loved, or to satisfy through a momentary fantasy the need to be cared for."

He also has some advice for parents whose children are engaged in what he calls "this kind of non-loving sexual involvement." He writes, "Perhaps some words of understanding or, if needed, reassurance will make a difference and head off or alter a sexual involvement that can only create more problems than it will solve."

As for girls, he says, "It is to no girl's advantage to develop a bad reputation. A girl who persists in pursuing sexual behavior that is damaging to her reputation (regardless of how "unfair" the double standard may be) is operating out of motives that have very little to do with sex as a pleasurable experience."[1]

THE COURAGE TO BE DIFFERENT

Dating for young teenagers today is difficult, to say the least, in a world that really attacks the very center and sanctity of the special way we look at sex.

The dating experience can be a rocky one with many hills and valleys. There will be tears and heartaches—days of incredible exhilaration followed by rapid plunges into dark depression. But if teenagers are able to develop friendships with other kids who believe as they do, if they realize that they are special, and if they don't want to get themselves into situations where they're being used or are using someone else, then I believe they can get through these tough times with minimal scrapes and scars.

I talked with one young man who told me that he had a best friend with whom he made a pact of purity.

"All of our friends were getting involved sexually," he told me, "and it didn't seem to matter who it was. When we asked one of the guys in our group why he was always after anyone or anything he could get, he said, 'It's better than masturbating.' That's all the respect they had for sex—or for the girls they were sleeping with."

Because he and his best friend didn't feel that way, they agreed that they were both going to "save themselves" for marriage. Does that sound archaic? Well, both of these boys were popular—one was the vice president of his senior class and the other was voted "Athlete of the Year" during his senior year. What's more, one of the "bad girls" in the school let it be known that her mission in life was to have sex with the athlete. She openly broadcasted her desire to "deflower" him, and let him know that she was ready whenever he was. But the young man believed strongly that sex was something that included a lifetime commitment between one man and one woman, and so he refused her offer of "the best time you've ever had." And because these two young men believed there was something "sacred" about sex, they supported each other, and they were both virgins on the day they graduated from high school. Yes, that's quite an accomplishment in these modern times, but it *can* be done.

What they had done was to fight the peer pressure to become involved in sex by creating a little peer pressure of their own to abstain from sex. There is much to be said for getting teenagers involved in the right groups, for encouraging friendships with kids who are going to support them and build them up rather than ridicule them and drag them down.

As I told a couple of parents not too long ago, our goal with teenagers is to be able to get them through the teenage years without them killing themselves or without someone else killing them! It's difficult to be different, especially when the whole peer group says everybody's got to be the same— and when that entire group is perched high up on a ledge overlooking 34th Street in Manhattan! But if your son or daughter really wants somebody special in life, if he or she really looks forward to marriage as being something unique where two people really do come together and become a single entity within themselves, then he is going to have to have the courage to be different, to say no when it's the best choice, and to be very selective about whom he dates and with whom he associates.

HAZARDS OF PREMARITAL SEX

I've already said a bit about premarital sex, but as a marriage and family counselor I feel I must say more. There's a great deal of pressure on teenagers to engage in sex, and this comes not only from the peer group but from society in general. Kids are being forced to grow up too soon, and to complicate matters, every place they look they are being bombarded through the media with all different forms of sexuality. Advertisers have learned that sex sells everything from cars to clothes to soft drinks.

I'm sure you've heard some of the statistics about the problems that are brought about by young people engaging in intercourse before they're married, but let me refresh your memory:

1. The Danger of Children Having Children
Birth control devices are everywhere, and they're relatively easy to obtain. There are condoms, birth control pills, diaphragms, all sorts of things, and the law makes it possible for teenagers to obtain many of them without their parents' knowledge.

So how come more than one million women—the majority

of them teenagers—become pregnant outside of wedlock in the United States every year? And with all of these birth control devices available, why are we aborting hundreds of thousands of unwanted babies every year?

Now I don't know how you feel about abortion, but let me tell you that I think we've really overstepped some line of logic if we begin to think that it's nothing more than another form of birth control. It's not. It's one thing to prevent a pregnancy from taking place, and quite another to terminate a pregnancy once it has already occurred. Abortion can lead to long-lasting psychological scars, especially if the person who undergoes an abortion is a teenager.

And of course there are terrible problems awaiting the teenage girl who decides to keep her baby. According to *The New York Times,* the United States reached the point in 1985 where 20 percent of all births in this country were to women who were not married. *The Times* reported then that the number of births to unwed women had been increasing steadily for several years, and I've seen nothing since then to make me believe that the trend is headed in the other direction.[2]

The experts tell us that part of the reason for the continuing growth in the number of teenage pregnancies is that many teenagers don't use birth control devices, even though they know such devices are available to them.

There are several reasons for this. The first is very difficult for adults to understand, but the truth is that many a young woman who feels alienated and unloved by the significant others in her life—her mom and dad and her family—might really want to get pregnant.

The fantasy of having her own little baby sounds wonderfully attractive to a young teenager who feels that life has dealt her an unfair hand of one kind or another. She thinks it will be good to have a baby to hold and cuddle—somebody she can love unconditionally and who will love her in the same way. But she doesn't stop to think of the responsibilities that a baby brings with it. A baby is not a puppy or a stuffed animal—and too many girls don't find that out until it's too late.

Such teenage naïveté is exceeded only by stupidity. It's only after the adolescent has given birth to a child that she begins to realize the awesome responsibilities she has incurred by choosing to get pregnant. So then, though it's a common assumption that young men are always looking for the "easy score," let it be known that there are also many young women who are looking for just the right young man to father their first child.

I know of one situation right now where the extremely rebellious daughter committed what, to her, must have been the ultimate act of rebellion—becoming pregnant. When she announced to her parents that she was going to have a baby she did so with a defiant tone, without the slightest hint of worry or remorse. She also told them that she was going to keep the baby and there was nothing they could do about it.

She was 14.

When the parents went to the department of social services they found out that their daughter was correct. Even though they wanted her to put the baby up for adoption, they could not force her to do so. The law said that if she wanted to keep the baby, she *could* keep the baby. Meanwhile, though, Mom and Dad were obligated to support their daughter, and their grandchild—at least until the girl had reached her 18th birthday.

So now the girl is nearly 16, she's trying to go to school, hold down a job, and care for her child. She's finding that her rebellion had dire consequences for herself, her parents, and her child. As time has gone by, she's come to realize that once you've decided to become a mother you're going to be a mother for the rest of your life. It's not something you can step into and then step back out of as if you're putting on an overcoat. As a result, she has exhibited some signs of resentment toward the child—nothing overt—but the fact is that she's not mature enough to be caring for a baby, and that is showing in her behavior. As far as Mom and Dad are concerned, they have learned to love their grandchild, but the presence of the baby in their home has changed their lives. They were at the point where they were beginning to think about the things the two of them would do together once their children had left the nest, and now the presence of the baby in the family has completely altered all their plans. And I won't get into the battles they've had trying to get the father, a high school junior whose only income is his allowance, to provide some support for the child he helped bring into the world.

An unwanted pregnancy is not beneficial to *anyone*.

One reason why many girls might not use birth control methods is that they were brought up with traditional Judeo-Christian values. In this case, using birth control would indicate that they were planning to sin or to go against God's laws. Thus it would be a guilt-producing experience to use a birth control device. I recall one young woman of 16 who was sexually active with her boyfriend, who was 18. Although the young man wanted to practice contraception by use of a condom, she wouldn't let him. She said she felt it would violate her religious practices. (Psychologically, as long as she could avoid the reality that she was actually choosing to be sexually active and accepting the responsibility for that choice, she could claim innocence by saying, "It just happened.")

I suppose the most obvious reason teenagers don't practice birth control is that many of them simply don't live a very structured or planned life. In the process of not taking the time to think about what their physical and sexual limits are in the dating relationship, many teenagers find themselves in situations where one thing just leads to another. In the height of passion it's very difficult and cumbersome to take time out and use contraceptives of any kind. There is a tendency on the part of some teenagers to be so caught up in the fantasy of lovemaking that they don't want any interruptions, even an interruption that is designed to protect themselves from pregnancy. Did you ever see a movie where, during one of those titillating love scenes, the young lovers stopped to use a contraceptive? It just doesn't seem like the romantic thing to do.

You know by now that I believe the best method of birth control is abstinence. It's certainly the only method that's 100 percent reliable. But if you know your child is going to become sexually active, or if you suspect that your child is sexually active, you need to have a frank talk with him or her about the need for preventing an unwanted pregnancy. Some parents don't want to talk about birth control with their teenagers because they don't want to face the fact that their children might be active sexually. Some teenagers will flat-out lie and tell their parents that they're not sexually active because they know that's what Mom and Dad want to hear. But I would rather have my child using contraceptives than to have him or her playing a game of "sexual Russian roulette."

Lawrence Bauman says, "A teenage pregnancy means the end of childhood. Whatever plans the girl, or implicated boy, may have had, an unexpected pregnancy introduces a drastic change of course. Thus, good advice, I think, is for parents to sit down with their children *prior* to a pregnancy —and that usually means prior to sexual intercourse—for a frank discussion of how to avoid becoming pregnant.

"Discussing with your child the dangers of pregnancy and the various ways of preventing pregnancy does *not* necessarily mean that you are condoning sexual intercourse by your teenager. If you feel that your child is not ready for a full sexual relationship, you can tell your child this. It may even surprise you to find out that your child respects your opinion, and has been just waiting for you to make it known. On the other hand, if your child is determined to have a sexual relationship, regardless of your approval or disapproval, it is far better that the child should be advised on how to take steps to avoid a pregnancy than to simply go ahead willy-nilly without precaution."[3]

2. The Danger of Disease.

A few years ago, everyone was worried about herpes. And while herpes is still a very real problem, its danger has been overshadowed by something even worse. I am, of course, talking about AIDS—acquired immunodeficiency syndrome. Herpes is a nuisance—often a painful nuisance—but AIDS is a killer.

AIDS is a terrible problem, and it's made worse for teenagers by the fact that many of them believe, "Oh, I could never get AIDS. I'm not a homosexual, I don't use intravenous drugs, and I've never had a blood transfusion, so what do I have to worry about?"

Well, the truth is that you don't have to be a homosexual, an intravenous drug user, or have a blood transfusion to get this deadly disease. Your teenager needs to know that when he is having sex with someone he is, in effect, having sex with everyone that person has had sex with, at least during the last five years. All that needs to happen is for one infected person to get in there somewhere, and the result can be disastrous.

I don't want to sound alarmist when it comes to talking about AIDS, but the truth is that it is a very real danger, and if your teenager is going to be sexually active, he needs to know the sexual history of his partner or partners.

A friend of mine recently returned from a trip to the African nation of Uganda. He told me that Uganda is a beautiful place—that parts of the countryside are breathtaking. But this is a nation ravaged by AIDS—with perhaps as much as half the population infected. He asked one shopkeeper if his family had been touched by AIDS—and in answer the shopkeeper took him around to the back of his business. There were nine graves, each containing the body of a relative who had succumbed to the disease, and the shopkeeper broke down and cried.

What has happened in Uganda and other African nations gives testimony to the fact that AIDS is not confined to the homosexual or drug-addict segments of the population. On the other hand, it is true that those who do not put themselves at risk are not likely to contract the disease. Would I ostracize someone who has AIDS the way the residents of his hometown ostracized the heroic Ryan White, who contracted AIDS through no fault of his own and who eventually died from the disease? Of course not. I am not afraid to associate with people who have AIDS, because I know that the disease cannot be transmitted by casual contact. But at the same time, I would be very cautious about whom I was sleeping with and realize that here, as in every other situation having to do with teenage sex, abstinence is the very best policy.

How does AIDS work? It cripples the body's disease-fight-ing immune system and leaves its victims vulnerable to a variety of life-threatening infections and even certain cancers. AIDS is primarily transmitted through sexual contact, although it can also be transmitted by contaminated blood transfusions or the sharing of contaminated hypodermic needles. It can also be passed from a mother to her child at or before birth.

According to the Centers for Disease Control in Atlanta, more than 100,000 Americans have contracted AIDS, and more than half of those have already died from the disease. It is estimated that more than 1.5 million Americans carry the AIDS virus, and that 1 in 30 men between the ages of 20 and 50 are infected.[4]

It is true that AIDS is primarily found among those who are homosexuals, and if you have reason to believe that your child has developed homosexual tendencies, then by all means talk to him about the danger of AIDS. I won't get into the "rightness or wrongness" of homosexual behavior here, because it's not really my intention to cover that in this book. Suffice it to say that homosexual activity can lead to numerous problems, the worst of which is acquired immunodeficiency syndrome. The big talk now is "safe sex" for homosexuals and heterosexuals alike, and that means, primarily, the use of condoms. But condoms do not always work as a preventative for pregnancy, venereal disease, or AIDS. And as I have said before, I believe that passing out condoms to teens is like issuing them squirt guns to fight a forest fire. Why rely on devices that are far from 100 percent effective to combat a disease that is 100 percent fatal?

What should teenagers know about AIDS?

• It can be transmitted through heterosexual intercourse.

- It may be transmitted through oral sex, or deep kissing.
- The more sexual partners you have, the greater your risk of contracting AIDS.
- The best protection against AIDS is abstinence.

As I write this there is no known cure for AIDS, despite the fact that millions of dollars have been pumped into research aimed at finding one. The disease is still claiming thousands of lives every year and shows no signs of slowing down.

Now AIDS is terrible, but don't forget that there are other diseases out there, too.

In an article titled "Did He Leave You with More Than a Memory?" the author says that there are more than 20 sexually transmitted diseases. Of these, five must be reported to the Department of Health by your doctor because they are so hazardous to health and are highly contagious. The five are: syphilis, gonorrhea, chancroid, granuloma inguinale, and lymphogranuloma.[5] That article was written way back in 1980, and since then there are three other diseases to add to the list. These are: nongonococcal urethritis, genital herpes, and trichomoniasis.

In their book *You and Your Adolescent,* Dr. Laurence Steinberg and Ann Levine point out that an estimated eight million Americans are suffering from gonorrhea, and that there are three to ten million new cases of chlamydia each year. What's more, some 75 percent of the victims of sexually transmitted diseases are between the ages of 15 and 24.

They point out that AIDS is not the only dangerous sexually transmitted disease: "For girls untreated gonorrhea and chlamydia can lead to pelvic inflammatory disease, or PID (an infection that spreads from the vagina or cervix, through the uterus, into the fallopian tubes and sometimes to the ovaries). PID is dangerous in itself and may also cause sterility. In boys, untreated gonorrhea and chlamydia can cause problems with urination, difficulties getting an erection, and sterility. The couple are not the only ones who are affected. If a woman who has either of these STDs (sexually transmitted diseases) gets pregnant, she may have a miscarriage or stillbirth, or her baby may be born with infections serious enough to cause blindness."[6]

3. The Danger of Ignoring the Statistics.

Way back in 1965, about 10 percent of female high school students and 25 percent of male high school students reported that they were sexually active. Times have changed. The most recent figures I've seen indicate that in today's high school's one-half of the boys and nearly one-third of the girls are "sexually active." (And I'm not talking about an isolated sexual experience, but about boys and girls who engage in sexual relations on at least a semi-regular basis.)[7]

Further statistics I have seen indicate that by the time they are 19 years of age, only one-fifth of all boys and one-third of all girls have not engaged in intercourse. And as we've already talked about, thousands upon thousands of them are becoming pregnant every year, many of them as young as 13 or 14 years old.

According to an article entitled "Adolescence and Sexual Behavior" by Dr. Kevin O'Reilly and Dr. Sergi Aral, printed in the *Journal of Adolescent Care,* as of the mid-1980s teenagers accounted for nearly one-third of all abortions performed in the United States each year.[8]

What do you do when you hear statistics like these? If you're like most parents you think, "Isn't it terrible what other people's kids are up to?"

We tend to think statistics don't apply to us until they hit home.

If you want to see to it that your child doesn't become a statistic with regard to pregnancy, abortion, or venereal disease, the very best thing you can do is keep the lines of communication open. Sometimes kids get the idea that their generation is the first one to find out about sex. Or else they think that surely Mom and Dad have forgotten most of what they knew about it by now. (They certainly can't picture their parents ever engaged in lovemaking!)

Let them know that you know all about it, that you understand how they feel and the pressures they're facing, and you've taken a big step in the right direction.

Are you brave enough to take the responsibility to open up and talk to your teenager? Let's face it—it's difficult to talk to anyone about sex—and even more difficult to talk about it with your own son or daughter. But teenagers need their parents to make a commitment to get involved in their lives, to help them navigate through the turbulent waters of adolescent sexuality.

I can't think of a better way to become involved with your teenagers than to share some real life experiences that may not only show your teenagers that you're not really the product of the Dark Ages, but that you do realize the many struggles and temptations they face. When you are brave enough to share some experiences from *your* life, then your teenager might be brave enough to share *his* real thoughts and feelings with you.

Perhaps you'll want to plan a weekend trip together— where you'll go fishing, camping, swimming, or engage in some other activity, and where you'll have plenty of time to talk about things that are really important.

I realize that you're probably thinking, "Oh, sure. My teenage son would just love to go away with Mom and Dad." But remember, you have to learn to walk before you run. If you have difficulty communicating with your teenager, I suggest that you begin to make some inroads in this area by taking your teenager out for lunch or dinner. Let him choose the restaurant. Then, after you have made a few attempts to establish intimacy, plan a family weekend away together, or perhaps a weekend with one of your children and yourself.

If the thought of a heavy conversation with your teenager is scary to even think about, start off with something light. Have you ever told them some of the crazy, foolish, dumb, or even weird things you did as a teenager? Don't try to fool me by looking dignified, I know the types of things you did when you were a kid. We all did. So why not share some of those things and show your children—who think you attended school with Thomas Edison and Benjamin Franklin—that you really were a kid at one time, and that it hasn't been so long ago that you've forgotten what it was like.

Think for just a moment about where you got all of your information about sex. Didn't you get it from other misinformed friends? Or from dirty stories or restroom walls? Research tells us that very few people are privileged enough to get a good, honest dialogue going with their parents. No wonder so many teenagers are statistics waiting to happen.

You *must* talk to your teenagers, and the sooner the better because *now* is the time to start.

I know that you may have a busy schedule. It may be hard to find the time and/or the money for a weekend trip. But remember that how you spend your time and money is a reflection of your priorities. If your children are a high priority in your life, then you're certainly going to be spending your time and money on them. My own schedule is extremely hectic, yet I've taken my children, one at a time, out

99

of school to go on business trips with me when I'm conducting a seminar or doing a television program in another city. It's a very unique time that we have together. We have fun and we laugh, but more importantly we have some time for just the two of us, and I know that my children look forward to these times together. They would literally forsake any of their own activities to hop on an airplane and go with me—and we always come back home closer and with a better understanding of each other.

LIVING TOGETHER

No discussion of teenage sexuality would be complete without a discussion of the couple that decides to live together without benefit of marriage. We used to call this "shacking up," and it wasn't the sort of thing to be discussed in polite company.

But here again, times have changed. It has become more and more acceptable. That may be primarily due to the influence of Hollywood, where it's not uncommon to find that cohabitation and the birth of children have nothing at all to do with marriage.

It seems like I'm always hearing statements out of Hollywood along the lines of, "We're so happy that we're expecting our third child, and we may even talk about marriage one of these days."

Well, even though we've accepted "living together" as a normal arrangement, I really don't think it should be considered the norm, and I say that primarily because of the experiences I've had in dealing with couples who thought this would be the best way to go.

Kay and John were a typical example of the couples I see

100

in my private practice so often today. They were in their early 20s, had lived together for about two years, and then they decided to get married. The day after their wedding, things began to disintegrate. All of a sudden they were confronted with problems that never existed when they were living together. They were legitimately confused and puzzled when they came for therapy. I say they're typical because John and Kay and thousands of other couples just like them made a judgment error. They really thought that living together was a foolproof way to test whether or not they were compatible for marriage.

You really can't blame them for thinking along those lines. It does seem to make sense, on the surface, that living together would be a good way to find out if a relationship will work. But it isn't. Why not? Because there's a key element missing in a relationship of this kind, and that element is one of the most important ingredients in any marriage: Commitment.

There is no commitment between two people who are just "playing house."

Living together is really the heaviest form of dating, and that means that couples who just live together never really take off their masks. They are always on their best behavior, and basically afraid to just relax and be the people they really are.

Living together is a commitment not to make a commitment. The couple who lives together has an open-ended agreement with each other. In a marriage, however, the commitment to each other is made in front of the whole world, and is "till death do us part." It's not something to be taken lightly.

We live in an age when commitment is not a valued commodity. But when it comes to that true intimacy that so many young men and women apparently yearn for, there is no other way to get it than by committing to each other, and that means marriage.

No, the success of a marriage will not be enhanced one bit by living together before that marriage.

There are also other practical considerations that make me recommend against such an arrangement—such as very little financial protection, no security, no retirement benefits, and few other legal protections in general. Yes, we've all heard the news stories of women who were jilted by their big-name lovers and who were awarded hundreds of thousands of dollars via their "palimony" suits. But those "success" stories are the exception rather than the rule, and there is very little in the way of security in a live-in relationship.

In addition to these practical reasons, another thing for a young woman to consider are the emotional scars that remain throughout her lifetime. On the basis of my working with hundreds of couples during the past decade I have come to the conclusion that it is generally true that women tend to carry the emotional scars of a breakup longer than men do. She is especially likely to carry the pain of the breakup if she feels that she "gave herself" to someone who wasn't worthy of her—or who wasn't really the person she thought he was.

For many women, guilt associated with living together prior to marriage is an added burden that they must carry through life. Even though they intellectualize things and may tell you that they felt perfectly fine about the arrangement, underneath they tend to feel very guilty for what they have done. This is because they feel that they have rejected their parents' standards and values—or perhaps their own standards and values. Either way, when a "living-together" arrangement falls apart, it is generally the woman who suffers, and that's why I think the young woman is smartest who remembers that there is truth to the old cliché: "Why buy the cow when you can get the milk for free?"

I don't mean to be flippant or vulgar about it, but if a man has all the benefits of marriage without any of the responsibilities, then why should he bother with marriage? My advice to any young woman who is being pressured by her boyfriend to move in with him is to tell him that she'll be glad to do it—after the preacher says, "I now pronounce you husband and wife."

LEARNING SOME LESSONS

Because I think it would be beneficial, I'm going to share with you a transcript of remarks from one of my clients. Chuck, who came to me in his early 20s seeking direction for his life, gave me permission to pass this on because he hopes someone will be helped by his experiences:

"Premarital sex is something I would never have dreamed I'd be talking to anyone about because, along with alcohol and dope, as I was going through school, sex was also the thing to do. . . . It wasn't really until I'd grown up a little bit that I found out just what kind of adverse effect premarital sex has. Especially for the woman. I hate to say that; I hate to sound biased, but especially for the woman.

"I have a good friend who shared how she and her boyfriend were madly in love. They just knew they were the right ones for each other. They engaged in premarital sex— she gave herself to him literally, because in sex the two really do become one. Premarital sex puts a strain on a relationship because the relationship then becomes just physical. Instead of meeting and talking, sharing your day, going to a movie, just enjoying being with each other, you get together, have sex, and leave. Just to fulfill your needs, you might say.

"Anyhow, this friend and her boyfriend, after a couple of months, found out that they weren't right for each other; they weren't meant to get married. She's twenty-one years old, a college graduate and a beautiful girl. As she told me about this I could see in her eyes the hurt she had gone through. She said she would wake up in the morning and vomit blood because she was so upset. She had given herself to somebody and he wasn't the right person, and she couldn't get back what she had lost. It's kind of like giving someone a million dollars and later finding out you gave it to the wrong person, but now he's gone and so is your money. Gone for good. You don't have it anymore. And the person who should have had it will now never get it.

"I recently started going out with a girl that I knew a few years ago. One thing I admired back then, really liked and respected about her, was that she wasn't messing around with anybody. Even when I was messing around with drugs and alcohol I still had a high ideal of what I wanted in a girl, and this girl was my kind of woman because she didn't give in to guys. Well, after I changed my lifestyle, this girl came back into my life. We started going out to dinner and talking and sharing our lives. It was just beautiful. She was just as lovely as she was the day I first met her.

"One day she shared some experiences she was struggling with. She said that she had made love with this guy. She looked at me and said, 'Chuck, if there is some way I could turn back the hands of time . . .' I don't think this guy was worried about it, but I can guarantee you she was. He had given her the ultimatum that 'if you love me you will,' and she did, so she did. She never felt right about it and it really had a traumatic psychological effect on her.

"Then when we were having dinner one night she told me about another guy. She thought she was going to marry him and lived with him for two years while she went through college. I can't tell you what her telling me that did to me. It was like a slap in the face. Here was this girl I thought was so special, that I had such high regard for, telling me that she lived with somebody for two years. For some reason that just didn't set with me right. I had hoped that the woman I would fall in love with and marry would share all the little deep secrets of her mind, her feelings, and her philosophy with me. I think when you're lying in bed with different people all of the time it's kind of hard to know who's special and who's not. Don't get me wrong. She wasn't laying around with a lot of different people, but living two years with a guy, a lot of things can happen between them.

"But when I talked with Dr. Leman about this he explained to me that I had taken away a lot of those special things from girls I had sex with in high school. That really hit me. Some of those girls know in the back of their minds that they will have to share our experiences with the ones they fall in love with. I can imagine how those boyfriends are going to feel. I feel it once, but I might have caused it ten times.

"I know one girl who told me she doesn't hold or kiss or anything on a first date. By today's standards that's kind of hard to believe. She's a beautiful college girl; but she doesn't want to get trapped in any kind of a relationship until she gets married. She wants to keep all her dates on a friendship basis. I think that's neat."

THERE'S ONLY ONE RIGHT WAY

Darrell Royal, former University of Texas head football coach, once said that there were three things that could happen when you made a forward pass, and two of them were bad. So it is with sex.

Sex is for one man and one woman who are committed to each other. Not for teenagers who just want to "score."

It's hard to figure out why two 15-year-old girls would have a race to see who could lose her virginity first, but this was the case of one of my young clients and her girlfriend. They obviously didn't know very much about sex, including the fact that research strongly suggests that a woman's first sexual experience is not likely to be a satisfying one.

Katherine Bement Davis told of one study with 1,000 educated married women. That study found that one-fourth of them were repelled by their first sexual experience.[9]

There seems to be similar agreement along that line in many other studies. Paul Popenoe, director of American Institute on Family Relations, found that in a survey of 658 women, only 25 percent of them achieved a normal climax at first intercourse. Only seven percent achieved climax in the first 30 days, an additional 26 percent between one and eleven months. Some 16 percent had their first orgasms a year or more after becoming sexually active, and six percent reported never being able to attain orgasm.[10]

My 15-year-old client reported to me that her first sexual experience "hurt like hell." Her date was very drunk, left her in the park, and drove himself home. In many circles of young people today it really is a cool thing to lose your virginity, and the earlier the better. This young girl won the race all right, but what a price she had to pay.

One of my observations about people is that they always

106

seem to want what they can't have. A teenage girl who refuses to let her body be used, who doesn't follow the crowd in the sexual contests, but seems to be a little different from everyone else, is a cut above all the rest. She truly is someone worth dating, pursuing, admiring, and caring for.

Sex is a gift, and teenagers can accept that gift. That's the easy part. The hard part is to make wise decisions concerning the use of that gift. Teenagers need to keep themselves out of situations where they are abused in any way, shape, or form. They need to be taught that people are for loving and things are for using, instead of the other way around. It's important to teach our adolescents that they are not to use others, nor are they to let others use them.

There will always be somebody who will gladly use others for his own satisfaction. There are plenty of such people "out there," and they are of both sexes.

The thing is that we have the freedom to decide how we're going to conduct ourselves. But as the Fram Oil Filter man tells us, we can pay now or pay later. We can follow the rules and enjoy life to the maximum or abuse them and pay for it the rest of our lives. It's our decision to make.

IT'S HARD TO WAIT

Anyone who knows me knows that I'm a fan of old-time rock 'n' roll. I love music from the fifties and sixties, and I even have a jukebox in our bedroom stocked with some of the greatest music that's ever been committed to vinyl. And you know, most of that music is loaded with teenage angst— with lyrics talking about the pain of being a teenager in love, about how difficult it is to wait for adulthood, and so on. In "I Think We're Alone Now," Tommy James and the Shondells sing about a young couple who have to sneak away to be alone because the grownups in their world won't let them be (and I know this theme is still popular because Tiffany had a number one hit with this same song a few summers ago); Paul Anka sings about the tragedy of two teenagers who are having their relationship put down as "Puppy Love"; the Beach Boys sing about the days when the couple can say good night and stay together in "Wouldn't It Be Nice?" and so it goes. It's always been hard for teenagers to be patient when it comes to sex and romance, and I guess it always will.

Especially when you know you've found the "love of your life," or at least think you've found the love of your life.

But when teenagers rush into a sexual relationship or marriage, almost without exception it ends up being a disaster.

Many young people have a great deal of ambition and determination. The girl admits the guy she's in love with has *a few* faults, but she thinks she can change him. She says "Oh, he's going to be different after we married." She figures he'll stop smoking dope, or drinking, or running around with other women, or that he'll find a job, but she's living in a fantasy world.

There's no way that any of us can change another person, not someone we're married to, or a son or daughter, mother or father. All we can do is change our own behavior, which might, in the long run—and sometimes that's a real long run —help the other person change his or her behavior.

Cheryl was one of those women who was determined that things would work out because she and Dave were in love. She knew he wasn't perfect, but figured that love would indeed conquer all, and she was certain that he'd transform himself into Prince Charming once they were husband and wife. But he didn't, and instead of becoming better, he seemed to be worse. That's why, after seven years of marriage in which she and her husband had grown farther and farther apart, she sought refuge in the arms of another man.

He, too, was married.

Their affair lasted for about a year and a half before she finally realized that her lover was never going to leave his wife for her. She had managed to become stuck in two traps at once. She was trapped in a marriage in which she had grown more and more distant from her husband, and now she had also become trapped in an affair that was tearing her up inside.

Today Cheryl is still trying to put the pieces of her marriage back together, but she isn't getting much cooperation from Dave. And even though she's absolutely guilt-ridden because of her affair with a married man, she is still very much in love with him.

As far as he's concerned, the affair is over and he's content to go on with his life. But Cheryl will never be the same.

I've heard it again and again. "If only I could get someone to listen to me, so they won't make the same mistakes I made."

Love isn't all hearts and flowers and being swept away by waves of emotion. Love is getting up at night and walking the floor with a sick baby so your spouse can get some sleep; love is working hard all week and then coming home and giving the paycheck to your wife because she knows best what bills need to be paid; love is faithfully paying those bills and finding forty-seven ways of fixing hamburger casseroles to stretch the budget; love is eating those forty-seven varieties of hamburger casserole without complaining.

What teenagers need to understand is that anybody can be loving and attentive and fun to be with when things are going well. But in marriage, as in life, things aren't always going to go well. There are going to be some rough spots in the road—that's just the nature of life on this planet. The ideal mate is someone who's going to stick by you when those rough times come and help to make them better—and not someone who'll turn on you at the first sign of trouble.

Unfortunately, love has a way of blinding teenagers to the realities of life. But if you, as a parent, have attempted to establish good communications with your adolescent child, you will be more likely to get him to pay attention to your wisdom.

UNREALISTIC EXPECTATIONS

Do you suppose that when a young couple walks down the flower-strewn aisle of the church on their wedding day that they're thinking about getting a divorce in a few years? No, I don't think so either. But statistics show that the average marriage today lasts just seven years. That's one of the reasons why it's so fundamentally important for us to understand the very temporary nature of early romantic love.

I think of Kathy and Ron who were married at age 16. Kathy was escaping from an unhealthy situation in her home —her father was abusive to her and she very much needed the comfort and "love" of a male. Ron also had an unhappy home life. His mother was an alcoholic, so he, too, was running away from life as he had known it. They were looking for Shangri-la, and mistakenly thought they had found it in each other's arms.

Unfortunately, all they found was more heartache. Their "love" for each other dissipated very soon after they were married. By the time she was 19, Kathy was divorced and had two young children.

These young people made a mistake in judgment that could have been avoided. They both had poor self-concepts and because of this they sought out people who they hoped would give them comfort and fill that void in their lives. Unfortunately, for that insecure young couple, when things got rough after they were married and they really needed to be able to communicate with each other, they simply didn't know how. And so they wound up going their separate ways.

TELL THEM ABOUT THE TIMES YOU'VE GOOFED

Now we all make errors in judgment and do foolish things, and hopefully we all learn from our mistakes. As parents, we need to try to pass along to children the benefit of what we have learned from the mistakes we've made. No, that won't prevent them from making mistakes of their own, but it may at least cut down on them.

It's not always easy to expose our weaknesses to our children because we want them to look up to us. We're afraid that if we admit some of the times we've goofed, they may not feel the same about us. But any caring parent who is forced to choose between helping his child and maintaining his glossy image is certainly going to choose helping the child.

I think of what happened when my daughters Holly and Kristin came with me one night to a softball game. This was several years ago when both of them were small, and I was a fast-pitch pitcher in a city recreation league. It was the first inning and I wasn't even in the ball game because it wasn't my turn to pitch. I was coaching first base, instead. Well, in the first inning the umpire made what I considered to be an unbelievably poor call on a pitch that was way out of the strike zone, and I yelled out, "You're crazy!"

He jumped out from behind the plate, took off his mask, and shouted at me, "What did you say?"

He asked, so I told him: "You're crazy!"

He said, "You're out of the ball game."

And I retorted, "Well, I'm out of the ball game, but you're still crazy."

The rules call for players to leave not only the field but the entire park when they're thrown out of the ball game. Needless to say, I was embarrassed. It was the first time I had ever been thrown out of a game of any kind, and I hadn't even been playing. I felt bad enough about getting ejected in front of my teammates and the people who had come to watch the game—but what made it even worse was that it happened in front of my two little girls, who were at the age where they were just about certain that Daddy could do no wrong.

But then again, they were more interested in the slides and swings on the nearby playground than they were in Daddy's game, and it was a relief to discover that they hadn't seen my altercation with the umpire.

"Come on, girls," I called to them. "We've got to go home."

They looked at me with astonished looks on their faces and Holly said, "Home! We just got here. Why are we going home?"

I didn't want to tell them why we were leaving so quickly, so I told them just to come on, that I was in a hurry. But they wouldn't let the matter drop, and when we got to the car they kept saying that word that every parent of small children learns to dread: "Why?"

Well, I found myself about to lie to my children, to tell them some kind of fish story, but I caught myself. I turned to my younger daughter and said, "Krissy, what happens when you talk back to Daddy?"

She looked at me with a puzzled expression, but finally said in a questioning tone of voice, "We get sent to our room?"

I nodded my head. "Yeah, that's right. Well, Daddy just talked back to the umpire and the umpire sent Daddy to his room."

My children understood that one perfectly. So perfectly, in fact, that the first thing they blurted out as we entered the door several minutes later was, "Mommy, Mommy, guess what? Daddy got kicked out of the ball game!"

So the lesson is, when *we* make mistakes, our kids can learn from them.

HELP THEM SET STANDARDS OF THEIR OWN

When it comes to sex, I think we also can help our children to form standards of their own. I acknowledge the fact that the standards they form might be different from yours. But, on the other hand, they very well may end up to be the same as yours. It's important to grant teenagers the right and the freedom to make those decisions concerning themselves. Being alone with a girlfriend or boyfriend is obviously a time when the teenager is on his own. He or she should realize that if their own standards are broken, they're going to feel guilty about it. You can also acknowledge to your child that there are going to be times when he'll wish he could indulge in sexual pleasure. There are going to be temptations, and the temptations are very natural. But the

113

question is, are your teenagers going to allow their emotions to control their behavior, or are they going to consciously control their emotions.

When we don't act responsibly, if we abuse the gift of sex by treating it with a so-what attitude, someone's going to end up paying for it. Unfortunately for women, they seem to get the dirty end of the deal more often than men. Let's face it—women bear the children and are often saddled with the responsibilities of both motherhood and fatherhood while, more often than not, the man goes along on his merry way.

One evening I was addressing a group of athletes on the topic they had asked me to speak on—sex. I told them as best as I could from my experience of working with young people that, although it was very difficult, it was best to abstain from sex until they were married. Well, I must admit that I felt as if I were talking to a brick wall. I didn't sense much support. I was sinking fast and was about to run out of words and throw in the towel when I saw a hand go up in the back of the room.

In front of about 60 fellow athletes this young man named Dave got up and said, "You guys know Sherry and me. You know that we've been going together for almost three years. I want to share something with you that Dr. Leman just said that really hit me right between the eyes. Six months ago Sherry and I made a commitment, or recommitment, I should say. We were very active sexually. We love each other very much and, as you know, we're planning a summer wedding."

About this time I knew something was coming that was going to be good and powerful; I was all ears, just sitting back like the rest of the guys, listening. You could've heard a pin drop as Dave went on to say that he and Sherry made the decision six months before to quit having sex. He said, "I want to tell you guys that our level of intimacy has gone up 100 percent since we stopped having sex."

That young man finished up the evening for me. I didn't have to say another word. I concluded my talk at that moment and went to an informal time of sharing and answering questions. What a joy it was to see that young man get to his feet and say what he did. I'm sure it wasn't easy for him to get up and expose the intimacies of his life with his fiancée in front of 60 athletes, but he did, and that made the difference.

TAKE ACTION

• Do you know what your teenager's attitude about sex is? If not, ask him. Also ask him what his friends think about sex. Do they push him (or her) to become sexually active? It may be awkward to get the answers to these questions, but it's important to at least open the door so the two of you can communicate on the subject. Within the next week, commit yourself to discussing sex with your adolescent, even if you feel awkward and clumsy when you first approach the subject.

• Does your child know how you feel about sex? Let him know how you feel about it. For example, if you have strong religious beliefs, and think that sex should be reserved for marriage, discuss those beliefs with him. Don't think that he has automatically picked up on your values. It could very well be that he honestly doesn't know where you stand.

• There are several good books explaining in an effective and humorous way why unmarried teenagers should not engage in sexual intercourse. Check your local bookstore and see if you can find a book that is appropriate for your teen. But, after you buy such a book, don't just give it to your child and run in the other direction. You need to read it, too, and be prepared to initiate discussion about it.

• Play a game of "imagine." What would happen to your teen if she became pregnant, or if he made someone pregnant? How would his life change? What things would he miss out on doing? By discussing a hypothetical situation, your teenager will get a better understanding of what *could* result from sexual activity.

1. Lawrence Bauman, *The Nine Most Troublesome Teenage Problems and How to Solve Them* (Secaucus, N.J.: Lyle Stuart, Inc., 1986), p. 180.
2. Article in *The New York Times,* October 20, 1985.
3. Bauman, p. 181.
4. Centers for Disease Control, Atlanta.
5. "Did He Leave You with More Than a Memory?" *Mademoiselle,* August 1980, p. 106.
6. Laurence Steinberg and Ann Levine, *You and Your Adolescent* (New York: Harper & Row, 1990), pp. 248–250.
7. Douglas H. Powell, *Teenagers: When to Worry and What to Do* (Garden City, N.Y.: Doubleday and Co., 1986), p. 93.
8. Dr. Kevin O'Reilly and Dr. Sergi Aral, "Adolescence and Sexual Behavior," *Journal of Adolescent Care,* 1985.
9. Alan Guttmacher Institute as quoted in *People,* May 4, 1981, pp. 56–60.
10. Alan Guttmacher Institute, *People.*

5

A Four-Letter Word Called Love

Okay, now that we've talked about dating and sex, let's move on to something that's really tough.

Love.

That's right love. The emotion that makes the world go round. The emotion that can break your heart.

I suppose we've all been in love one time or another, but if someone asked us to tell them what love is, most of us would be hard-pressed to come up with an answer.

"Dad . . . how do you know when you're in love?"

"Uh . . . maybe you should ask your mother."

That's how most of the fathers I know would respond to that sort of question—and I don't blame them, because it's tough to come up with a good answer.

Is love butterflies in the stomach? Is it the pounding of your heart when you're close to that somebody special? Is it a blissful dizziness that comes over you when you hear *her* speak your name?

Parents, do you remember when you first fell in love? There's not a feeling like it in all the world. Now, let's see, the first six times I fell in love, some of the things I remember are the excitement of having a girlfriend, the thrill of giving her a friendship ring, and the disappointment at learning that she left it in her jeans' pocket and it got totaled in the wringer washing machine.

(But I couldn't be too mad, since I had dropped *her* ring down the bathroom sink.)

I guess I did fall in love six or seven times, and every time seemed a little bit more wonderful than the first.

But, of course, the love I'm talking about is the kind of love that Paul Anka sang about (and later on, Donny Osmond), "Puppy Love." Everybody falls in puppy love. Even your parents did, at one time. So here again is an opportunity for you to dig into your memory bank and tell your children about some of the happy moments—and even the not-so-happy moments—you had during your puppy-love experiences in your adolescent years.

I believe it really helps if we can tell our kids, prior to their adolescence, that they are probably going to experience some of the same things we experienced. Somebody is going to come into her life who is so special she can't wait until morning to see him again at school. He's going to walk around the corner one of these days and come face-to-face with the most beautiful girl he's ever seen.

Puppy love makes young men all of a sudden become compulsive about brushing their teeth and combing their hair, and sneaking a little bit of Dad's after-shave or cologne. (Did I say "a little bit"? You can generally recognize the teenage boy who's in love by the fact that his cologne gets to school 15 minutes before *he* does!)

Puppy love also makes the young girl stand in front of a mirror practicing special smiles, trying to look cool and disinterested, or combing her hair to perfection so that Mr. Right will think it's naturally that way.

WHEN I FOUND LOVE

Let's go back now to the question we asked a few moments ago—namely, "what is love?" How do we know the difference between infatuation and real love.

In answer to that question, let me tell you about the day I met my wife. Of course, our meeting was more memorable than most because as I mentioned to you earlier, I met her in the men's room at the Tucson Medical Center—well, sort of.

I was a janitor and she was a nurse's aide. I knew there was something special about her from the very beginning. I had seen her on a few occasions around the hospital and a couple of times she had actually said hello to me—but I could never think of anything charming or clever to say in response. My "good morning" in response to her "hi" just wasn't going very far toward getting a relationship started—or even a friendship.

By the time our eyes met that fateful day in the men's room she was probably beginning to wonder if maybe I was just a little bit weird. Maybe I'd better explain.

Like I said, I was a janitor and I was cleaning the men's room. You know how the janitor puts one of those mobile trash barrels in the lavatory doorway to let everyone know he's working in there? Well, I was just emptying some trash into the barrel at the door when my wife-to-be came around the corner. Our eyes met and I blurted, "Do you want to go to the World's Fair with me?" (The World's Fair was in Seattle that year, so that gives you a clue as to how long ago this was.)

No, it wasn't the most clever opening line any guy has ever come up with, but at least it was something more than "good morning." And Sande responded just as one would expect. She said, "Pardon me?"

119

That's how we got going. I invited her to go out for a hamburger, and I ordered one McDonald's cheeseburger and cut it in half with a plastic fork. (Impressing her with my obvious ability to shower her with riches.) My stomach was so nervous that I couldn't even finish my half. I shook inside just looking at that woman—she was that special. Did I love her? No, not then. Nor did I really love her over the next few weeks as we got to know each other better than better.

Infatuated? You bet I was. There wasn't a moment that went by that I wasn't thinking about her, daydreaming, and hoping our relationship would continue to grow. But as time went by, that infatuation grew into a deep, mature love, and I came to know that I really *did* want to spend the rest of my life with this beautiful girl.

We both laugh about our "first date" now, when we remember that I couldn't even get half a cheeseburger down because my stomach was churning so. If you visited my home and watched me eat now, after being married to Sande for so long, you'd see that infatuation doesn't last. That warm, glowing, nervous feeling isn't always there. But, given time, infatuation can turn into real love. Our initial infatuation with each other grew into a steady, loving relationship with which we're both very happy. But that love grew to that point only by the process of sharing and giving, not through taking. I don't really consider myself "lucky" to have such a wonderful wife. Although I love her as friend and mother of our children, I really feel that our relationship is a special gift from God. We have both worked at nurturing, protecting, and cultivating that special gift.

Over the years, many philosophers, poets, and great lovers have tried to answer our question as to the nature of love.

But I have yet to find a better explanation of love than

something that was written in a letter nearly 2,000 years ago by one of the men who was instrumental in the growth of the Christian religion. His name was Paul, and he wanted to make sure that the people who made up the Christian Church in the city of Corinth understood what love was.

His words can be found in the Bible, in the 13th chapter of the book of 1 Corinthians, otherwise known as "the love chapter."

Even though Paul's words were directed at a specific Christian community, they cut across all boundaries of religion, time, and space and apply to all of humankind. You don't have to be a Christian to benefit from these thoughts on the subject of love—and I wish every teenager in the world (and their parents too) would read them.

Paul starts off by talking about two things that love always is—patient and kind. Then he lists several things that love never is—jealous, envious, boastful, proud, haughty, selfish, rude. Then he follows through with some words about what love does not do—demand its own way, act irritable or grouchy, hold grudges, or notice others' mistakes. He ends his description with what love does—rejoices when truth wins, is loyal no matter what, and always believes in, expects the best of, and defends the one who is loved.

Let's consider some of these aspects of love in more detail.

1. Love is patient.

Teenagers are not noted for their patience. They want the world and they want it now—whether it's a new CD player, a Nintendo system, or a lasting relationship with that good-looking girl down the block. We live in a time of instant everything—from instant coffee, to soup, to TV dinners. And if your TV dinner won't be ready fast enough for you by sticking it in a regular oven, you can always have it faster by using your microwave. So why not instant intimacy with dating? Because love is patient, that's why not. Love needs time to get to know the other person. True love can wait until marriage for physical intimacy. Any guy who tells a girl that she can prove her love by having sex with him doesn't have a clue as to what true love really is. He should be pointed in the direction of the nearest high bridge and wished a happy landing. Love is patient.

2. Love is kind.

We must be kind enough to recognize that the differences we see in our mates are assets in the relationship and not liabilities. We must focus on the positives in the relationship and minimize the negatives. We need to encourage each other in all things, to take the time to say, "Thank you, you were sweet to do this" or "I appreciate your saying that." Through our actions toward our own spouse, we should be showing our teenagers how to behave toward that special girl or boy.

If they begin the habit of being kind before they are married, chances are that they will continue to be kind to their mate after they're married. Kindness is essential to a good relationship.

Rebecca's mother was upset when she came home from one of her dates with her steady guy nursing a bruise that looked suspiciously like it had been caused by a fist. When she confronted her daughter about it, the girl broke into tears, insisting that "You don't understand! He really loves me! I just made him mad! He won't ever do it again."

Mom had a hard time getting her daughter to see the truth, but, thankfully, Rebecca was finally able to extricate herself from this abusive relationship. Love is kind. You don't abuse the one you love, either with words or with fists.

Not long ago, I found out that a young woman I know was very sick with the flu. She had gone off to her doctor's appointment, taking her two small children—ages two and four —with her, because her husband was "too busy" to watch them. When she got home from the doctor's office, she found a note from him on the dining room table. The note said, simply, "Gone fishing. See you later."

The woman had a fever, she had that achy feeling and those chills that accompany the flu. She felt like "death warmed over," but her husband had left her at home, not only to fend for herself, but to care for those two small children all by herself.

That guy doesn't know anything about love, because love is kind. It looks for ways to help out, and not for ways to shirk responsibility. It recognizes the needs of the other person and seeks to meet them.

Well, if I weren't a psychologist with years and years of training, I'd probably feel like punching that "unkind" husband in the nose.

You've heard the old saying I'm sure, "You always hurt the one you love." Maybe, for various reasons, that's true, but I can tell you that if you love someone you will never hurt them on purpose. If your teenager's "love" is unkind to him or her, he needs to end the relationship right now. If your teenager is unkind to the object of his desire, then he may be experiencing many feelings—infatuation, desire, possessiveness, jealousy, and so on—but love isn't one of them.

3. Love is never jealous, envious, boastful, proud, haughty, selfish, or rude.

Does your teenager feel threatened when one of the other

123

guys is talking to his girlfriend? Does she get a sick feeling when she sees one of her friends smile at him?

That's jealousy, and there is no room for jealousy in true love—only trust.

Teenagers need to learn to be truly glad for their boyfriend or girlfriend when he or she accomplishes something or gets some kind of recognition. If she gets better grades or a better paying job or makes the dean's list, does he feel envious? Or maybe he's the one who gets good grades, has the best job, or makes the dean's list. Did he boast about it to his true love? Was he unduly proud or haughty?

"Karen, aren't you on the cheerleading squad?"

"No . . . I dropped out. Justin didn't like me being on the squad."

"Why not?"

"I don't know. He just didn't like it. He wanted me to quit, so I did."

That's not love, because love rejoices in the success of the other person.

"Jay, how's that after-school job going?"

"Oh . . . I quit."

"You quit? Why?"

"Renee didn't like it. She said I was working too many hours and that we didn't have enough time to spend together."

That's not love either, because that's jealousy and envy. "I don't want you spending time at that job after school—I want you spending time with me!" There is no love contained in that sort of attitude.

Does your teenager listen to his girlfriend, or is his goal in life just to have her listen to him? A person who demands all the attention is usually the one who is boastful or proud.

Love is built around mutual respect. It is not a matter of "I want you to give to me," but a matter of "I want to give to you."

Parents, are you setting the example for your teenagers in your own marital relationship?

4. Love does not demand its own way, act irritable or touchy, hold grudges, or pay particular attention to the other's wrongdoing.

Love never "gets back" at the other or tries to "get even." Love never demands its own way. I think if I could pick one part of Paul's writings on love to measure all relationships with, I think it would be this one: Love does not demand its own way. The other person's feelings are more important. How do you stack up here with your husband or wife? Can your teenagers learn by watching you.

I've seen the situation many times in teenage relationships where the girlfriend thinks her boyfriend is flirting with someone so she decides to "show him" by doing the same thing with the guys. Or perhaps the guy has gone away for a few weeks during the summer, and the girl starts thinking about him and wondering what he's doing.

Suddenly it hits her. What if he's going out with other girls? What if he's holding their hands . . . or even *kissing* them? Why, how dare he? She'll show him. And so she purposefully sets out to get even, even though her poor schmuck of a boyfriend hasn't done anything wrong!

That's not love . . . but it happens all the time.

Love is not irritable or touchy. Now this is interesting because it's usually the little things about our loved ones that drive us up the wall. It's the way the wife clicks her fingernails when she's nervous, or the way the husband chews his food that starts making our blood boil—those little irritations that grow and grow until they threaten to drive us absolutely crazy. But love is not touchy, and it learns to overlook those little irritations, or to speak gently about them to the offending party, before they develop into overwhelming annoyances.

Teenagers and their dates often argue over some of the dumbest things, but true love overcomes all of that.

And true love does not hold grudges or notice the other person's mistakes. Puppy love, on the other hand, is a bone digger. It is good at looking back into the past, finding a fault, and throwing it up to a loved one. It seldom asks for or gives forgiveness. Real love forgives.

5. Love always rejoices when truth wins, is loyal no matter what, and always believes in, expects the best of, and defends the one who is loved.

A relationship that is not built on truth will never be a lasting relationship. A life built on anything other than total honesty is probably going to have all kinds of difficulties.

You've seen what happens when two people get married who have tried to hide their true selves from each other all during their dating relationship. All of a sudden, they find out that they're married to strangers.

She says, "Why are you acting like this? You never used to do this when we were dating?"

He says, "Yeah . . . and when we were dating, you loved *everything* I did!

This is why many a woman has realized, too late, that the man she has married has a drinking problem (or vice versa). During the courtship, the person with the problem did his very best to keep it hidden, because he didn't want to jeopardize the relationship. That means, though, that the entire relationship is built on dishonesty and deceit rather than on honesty and openness—and dishonesty is indeed a flimsy foundation.

Regarding loyalty, if we really love someone we will be loyal to him or her no matter what the cost. We will always believe in him, always expect the best of him, and always stand our ground in defending him.

What does all this mean? It means that love goes on forever, and perhaps the most critical test a relationship will endure is the test of time. I don't know how many times people have come to me for marital therapy and said, "We fell in love." Yes, they fell in love all right, and in the process they hit their heads and forgot what love is really like. They don't treat each other like they love each other. They don't do kind things for each other. They don't put the other's feelings first.

Now I will admit that there are times when we fail to live up to what we know to be true—but as I said, I wish that everybody in the world would read these words from the Apostle Paul and then seek to live by them. If every action taken were measured in the light of these words, all of the marriage counselors in the world would soon be out looking for new work, and there would be a lot fewer teenagers with broken hearts!

THE STAGES OF LOVE

The authors of several books have talked about the stages of love, usually listing them as: (1) romantic love; (2) friendship love; (3) agape love. A relationship between a man and a woman that is true love really requires all three of these, and not just one or two.

Romantic love is that sensual, sexual kind of love. It is

really reveling in the newness of a marital relationship. What a special kind of love this is, and what a special time it brings to the life of a man, woman, boy, or girl. But if a couple never gets past this first stage, if their relationship is based solely upon this kind of love, they're in trouble. There's not always much depth to romantic love, and when tough times come along it will tend to dissipate, like the morning fog in the warmth of the sun.

Friendship love needs to be developed. Prospective marriage partners should really be very best friends. They should talk to each other about everything. They should enjoy being together.

If you've read any of my other books, you may remember that I sometimes mention a scene from one of my favorite old movies, *Shenandoah*.

In this movie, Jimmy Stewart plays the father of a family trying to survive during the days of the Civil War. In the particular scene I'm referring to, a suitor has asked Stewart's permission to marry one of his daughters.

Now I don't know if I have the dialogue exactly right, but it goes something like this:

"Do you like her?"

"Like her? Sir . . . I love her."

"I didn't ask you if you loved her. I asked you if you liked her." He then goes on to explain that romantic love is one thing, but that unless it's built on friendship, it's not going to make it through the tough times.

"Yes, sir. I like her. I like her a lot."

Once that assurance has been given, the character played by Stewart gives the young suitor his blessing.

Smart man, that Jimmy Stewart.

Prospective marriage partners should ask themselves this question: If I found out that I didn't have much time left to live—if I had only a few days or weeks—would I want to spend that time with the one I've given myself to? If the answer is "yes" without any reservation, then you truly like the person, and that tells you that there's something of a more lasting nature to go along with the romantic love.

Agape love. This is the level of love that couples need to be continually striving toward. Agape love is sacrificial love, the love that helps us put the other's feelings first. Agape love is not going to be found on the first date, or the first year, or maybe even after the first five years of relationship. It has to be developed and nurtured.

When most people talk about love they're talking about a tinsel kind of love—a love that's not lasting, based primarily upon the sensual and the physical, and that's not real love.

As I write this, one of the most famous women in the world is planning to be married. For the eighth time.

Some people look at her and go, "Wow! Eight times! She really must know a lot about love."

No . . . I don't think so. She undoubtedly knows a great deal about romance, but I don't think she knows a thing about love. I don't intend to put her down. She may be a very nice person—but she still doesn't know anything about love, or about the commitment that says "till death do us part."

Who are your teenagers' role models? Do they understand that they should not pattern their lives after people like our eight-times-married celebrity?

LOVE AND SEX ARE NOT THE SAME

Don't worry. We're *almost* through talking about sex.

In the book *Dating, Waiting and Choosing a Mate* by H. Norman Wright and Marvin Inmon, is a chart that shows the difference between love and sex. The authors preface the chart by saying, "Often people associate sex with being intimate. But there is a difference. There are different types of intimacy. There is also a difference between sex and love. Some people say that they have loved another person when they have had sex with him. But that isn't necessarily true. Many people have sexual intercourse but love has nothing to do with what went on. Notice the differences between love and sex."[1] (See below)

The problem as I see it is that adolescents, particularly girls, need to realize that sexual intimacy is not an indication of love. Tell your daughter that she's not "proving" anything to him by giving herself to him, except that he's finally been able to get through her defense system.

As often as not, a girl will find out that as soon as she gives the guy what he wants, he hits the road in search of another conquest. I remember one young woman who had slept with her boyfriend to prove that she loved him, and then noticed immediately that his attitude toward her became cold and angry. When she asked him about it, his response was, "If you slept with me . . . how do I know you haven't slept with someone else."

He was almost angry that she had given in to him. His pure, sweet girlfriend wasn't so pure after all, and he began to wonder if she had been easy prey for one or two other guys too. Have you ever heard anyone ask the question, "Will you still respect me in the morning?"

Well, girls, chances are very good that he won't.

One of the solutions to this sort of problem is to determine who is good and who isn't, and more specifically, who is good *for you* and who isn't.

Several years ago, I worked with a young divorced woman

LOVE . . .	SEX . . .
. . . is a process; you must go through it to understand what it is.	. . . is static; you have some idea of what it is like prior to going through it.
. . . is a learned operation; you must learn what to do through first having been loved and cared for by someone.	. . . is known naturally; you know instinctively what to do.
. . . requires constant attention.	. . . takes no effort.
. . . experiences slow growth—takes time to develop and evolve.	. . . is very fast—needs no time to develop.
. . . is deepened by creative thinking.	. . . is controlled mostly by feel—that is, responding to stimuli.
. . . is many small behavior changes that bring about good feelings.	. . . is one big feeling brought about by one big behavior.
. . . is an act of will with or without good feelings—sometimes "don't feel like it."	. . . is an act of will—you feel like it.
. . . involves respect of the person to develop.	. . . does not require the respect of the person.
. . . is lots of warm laughter.	. . . is little or no laughter.
. . . requires knowing how to thoughtfully interact, to talk, to develop interesting conversations.	. . . requires little or no talking.
. . . develops in depth to sustain the relationship, involves much effort, where eventually real happiness is to be found.	. . . promises permanent relationship but never happens, can't sustain relationship, forever is an illusion.

who was interested in finding a new relationship. I said, "I know it's hard for a 27-year-old woman to meet men."

"Oh, no, it isn't," she replied. "My roommate meets guys all the time."

"Oh? That's interesting. Tell me how, because I have a lot of divorced or widowed women coming here who are looking for ways to meet a man."

She answered, "It's really simple. She just goes to a bar and buys herself a drink. Pretty soon some man will buy her another drink, and they just sort of talk."

I pressed the point further to see what transpired. Connie's roommate would end up either at her apartment or his and they would have sex.

I looked at Connie and asked, "You mean to tell me that she can meet a guy, let him buy her a cheap drink, maybe even two or three or five, and then within a two-hour period she's in the sack with the guy?"

She nodded.

"Connie," I said, "if that's what you call meeting people, you're kidding yourself. You can always meet people like that. But nothing permanent will ever come out of that kind of relationship."

FILLING A NEED

There is an amazing similarity between a 27-year-old divorcee and a 16-year-old adolescent girl. They are both vulnerable and very susceptible to being used. That's because both of them are starving for love, especially if they have had unsatisfactory relationships with their fathers. Unless they come to understand what they are doing and why, and make conscious efforts to change their behavior, they are likely to go through life looking for some kind of permanent relationship with males, only to come up empty and dry.

Parents, tell your daughter that if her boyfriend wants her to "prove" her love by having sex with him, she should ask the boy why he is not willing to "prove" his love by waiting until they are married for sex. True love has to be developed over time, and can't be proven by one act, or developed by one act.

Many a girl has given herself to her boyfriend because she was afraid that if she didn't she'd lose him—only to lose him anyway—along with her virginity and her self-respect.

Your daughter can find the kind of love that is lasting, satisfying, and meaningful if she demands time to develop it. Not only will she do herself a favor, but she will also be doing her boyfriend a favor by letting him know that she is too special to be used. Guys soon recognize who the special girls are, and they will seek them out as lifetime partners.

Not long ago, I was on my way home when I noticed the bumper sticker on the car ahead of me. It said, "Nice girls go to heaven, but good girls go everywhere." I admit that it's kind of clever, but it's not true. A "bad" girl may get invited to a few parties, she may get and give a few thrills in the backseat of a car. But she's not going to be the kind of woman a man wants to be his lifetime companion and the mother of his children. B. B. King sang "The Thrill Is Gone," and pretty soon that's what will happen to the girl with the reputation. The thrill will be gone, she'll be alone, and her life will be empty.

And if you think I'm stretching the point or being melodramatic, let me assure you that I've seen this sad situation more than a few times.

Someone once said that a woman gives herself to a man in order to be loved. I think there is much truth in that statement. But a girl should ask herself if she really feels loved when she's in the middle of sexual intercourse. Does she feel cared for after it's finished, or does she feel used? Almost all women tell me that the times when they feel loved are when they are caressed, treated with respect, and looked upon as special.

Several years ago, I clipped an Ann Landers column out of the newspaper. The paper's a little discolored after all this time, but the message it contains is as fresh and as true today as it was when it first appeared in 1981.

"Dear Ann: In a recent column someone wrote about a husband who was unable to perform sexually after a prostate operation. A penile implant was suggested.

"My husband has been impotent for three years (also prostate trouble) and he is only 59. We have a wonderful life together—in every way. The sexual aspect of our marriage is much more satisfying to me than it was with my first husband, a handsome and virile man who demanded sex seven nights a week and twice on Sunday. But he knew nothing about making love—for him it was purely a physical exercise, a highly impersonal act. There was never any caressing or words of endearment. He showed no interest in me beyond the fact that I was the vehicle for his bedroom acrobatics. Although he was very bright in other areas (an intellectual), his ignorance and insensitivity never failed to amaze me.

"I do not miss sexual intercourse in the least. I am completely satisfied with tender caresses and loving kisses. I adore being held close. Falling asleep in the arms of my beloved is my idea of heaven.

"Believe me, Ann, I wouldn't have that stud back for all the money in the world.—Had It Both Ways."

"Dear Both Ways: I wish a copy of your letter could be attached to every marriage license issued in the Western world. Since it isn't possible, perhaps it might help to leave this column on the pillow of the man who needs to see it.

"How strange that many males who consider themselves enlightened—even sophisticated—don't know the difference between having sex and making love.

"When women write to me about this problem I encourage them to communicate their feelings. Some men need to be told what is pleasing. And some women need verbal guidance, too. A mutually satisfying sexual relationship is not a gift—it is an achievement. And well worth the effort."[2]

THE TRAGEDY OF DATE RAPE

Pam had a big crush on Joshua, so she was thrilled when he finally asked her out for a date. She enjoyed the evening and didn't object when he drove his car down a darkened road on the outside of town, and pulled over to park in an area that was overshadowed by trees. Nor did she object when he slid over, put his arm around her, and pulled her close for a passionate kiss.

And another . . . and another. Pam thought she was in heaven. She had waited for this moment for so long.

She squirmed a bit when his hand touched her breast the first time, but she didn't object too strenuously because she figured it was just an accident.

But the second time there was no mistaking his intentions. He put his entire hand on her breast and began rubbing it.

Wait a minute! Pam wasn't opposed to kissing, but this wasn't what she had in mind.

She pulled away from him: "Josh . . . don't. . . ."

His response was to pull her back to him, cover her mouth with his, and begin working overtime with both hands.

Pam tried to pull away again, "Stop it . . . I mean it!" She tried to sound as forceful as possible, but more than anything else she was scared. It was obvious now what Joshua had on his mind, and he wasn't going to stop until he got what he wanted.

He practically tore her clothes off, and forced himself upon her, right there in the front seat of the car. She felt used, abused, violated. He was moaning in ecstasy while she was in incredible pain of both body and spirit, and all she could think of was that she wished she had a gun so she could kill him.

When he was finished, Joshua took her home and dropped her off, without so much as a single word.

The next day, he was astonished when he learned that Pam had filed charges against him.

"Rape?" he said. "That's ridiculous. I never raped her! She wanted it every bit as much as I did. Sure . . . she might have said 'no' a couple of times, but I could tell that she didn't really mean it. She was just trying to make it look like she wasn't *too* easy. And let me tell you . . . she enjoyed it!"

Now the case is preparing to go to court and it's his word against Pam's. Who is the court going to believe?

As far as Pam is concerned, it's going to be difficult to get up on the witness stand and tell the judge—and maybe even a jury—what happened on that night. It was hard enough to tell her parents what had happened.

She doesn't want to let Joshua get away with what he did,

but she's beginning to think that maybe she should just forget the whole thing.

Well, Pam is not alone. Hundreds of girls and women are the victims of date rape every year. Rape isn't a crime that's limited to strangers in masks, who climb in through bedroom windows to assault women. Very often rape is committed by boys and men who are very well known to the victims —by friends and lovers who simply won't take "no" for an answer.

Date rape has been happening for years, but it has only recently begun to gain widespread attention. That's because women are doing just what Pam did—they are speaking up about what has happened to them, and they are pressing charges.

Date rape has to do with love because it involves love and passion that has gone awry—it is love that demands its own way.

If you have a teenage son, be sure to explain to him that when a girl says no, she means no. There's no need to accuse him of improper behavior. Perhaps he is a gentleman who treats every young lady with respect. But it is still a good idea to talk to him about the trouble that can result if he has sex with a girl against her will. Most perpetrators of date rape don't set out to rape their victims. What usually happens is that they get "carried away," and have trouble applying the brakes. That's not an excuse for what happens —just an explanation. But rape, however it occurs, is a very serious crime and a very serious violation of another human being.

Make sure your son understands that.

If you have a teenage daughter, teach her that there are some things she can do to avoid date rape:

—First, she should understand that boys can get carried

away. Some girls think it's fun to lead the boys along, to tease them, and that's dangerous. A female may feel total satisfaction from holding and kissing, but that's just the warm-up insofar as the male is concerned. Tell your daughter, too, that a boy who has been drinking may find it especially difficult to control himself.

—The girl should know when and where to draw the line. She should make up her mind beforehand that there is a certain line which she will not cross, nor allow her date to cross, period. In other words, she needs to know her limits, and if the boy crosses them, to say something along the lines of, "I really do like you, but if you don't stop this, I'm going to leave!" And then, if he *doesn't* stop it, she should leave.

—She needs to make her intentions clear. If a boy invites her to his house to listen to records, and she knows that his parents aren't home, she should make it very clear that she is not interested in sex. And if the boy pushes her to give in to him, she should explain that she's simply not ready for sex, and leave it at that—which brings me to the next point.

—If her boyfriend invites her to his house to listen to records and she knows his parents aren't going to be home, she would be well advised not to go at all. In other words, tell your daughter not to put herself into a situation where it would be relatively easy for a boy to take advantage of her.

As Laurence Steinberg and Ann Levine write, "It is not a good idea (for a girl) to go to a secluded place, including her own home when no adult is around, with a boy she doesn't know very well or a boy who has been pressuring her. If she thinks she may be getting in over her head, she should be extra careful not to say or do things a boy might interpret as come-ons."

They also offer this advice, "If a girl who has been assaulted, by someone she knows or by a stranger, does not feel she can talk to her parents, she should speak to another adult she trusts (a relative, minister, or physician) or call one of the rape hotlines listed in the Yellow Pages. Such calls are confidential, and the people who answer are trained to help deal with the emotional as well as the physical aftermath of date rape."[3]

What does date rape have to do with teenage love? Obviously, it has nothing at all to do with true love. But love between males and females often has to do with sexual passion—and teenage boys and girls need to be aware that when those passions are allowed to rage out of control, terrible consequences can result . . . for both sexes.

Sex is a wonderful gift, and when used and developed *correctly* it can be very beautiful. But it is not the way to build a solid, lasting relationship. The very act of sex, which can bring new life and joy, can also, through misuse, bring destruction and devastation to many lives.

TAKE ACTION

Your "assignment" this chapter is to do some things for your spouse so that your adolescents will see some of the components of love.

1. Husband, how about fixing dinner for your wife? You may not be the world's best cook, but you can find a simple recipe that you can handle. Make sure she knows, and that the kids know, that you're doing this because you love her. At dinner, propose a toast to her (even if it's with a glass of milk) and tell her in front of the children why you love her as you do.

2. Wife, enlist your adolescents' help in doing something

special for your husband—send "I love you" balloons to his office, or ask them to help you whip up a batch of his favorite cookies. Likewise, tell him in front of them some of the reasons why you love him.

3. Decide that you will set aside some time every evening for time alone together. Show your kids that you consider your relationship to be a high-priority item—that you enjoy each other's company. An adolescent who is "in love" may feel that his mom and dad are "too old" and that they simply don't understand how he feels. Show him, by your behavior toward one another, that you do understand what love really is, and that you are very much in love with each other. Remember that children often model the behavior of their parents, and if you want your children to have a proper respect for and understanding of male-female relationships, you should do your best to model such a relationship.

Finally, if you are a single parent, discuss your singleness with your teenager. If you are divorced, for example, talk in as nonjudgmental a way as possible about some of the reasons why you were divorced. If you made some mistakes you don't want your children to make, tell them what you did wrong. If you were left single by the death of your mate, try to talk to your kids—if you haven't already done so—about the relationship you once had. I know it may be hard for you, but your kids will appreciate being brought into your confidence, and they will benefit from it.

1. H. Norman Wright and Marvin Inmon, *Dating, Waiting and Choosing a Mate* (Eugene, Oreg.: Harvest House Publishers, 1978), pp. 145, 146.
2. Ann Landers, "Love and Sex Not the Same," copyright 1981 Field Newspaper Syndicate.
3. Laurence Steinberg and Ann Levine, *You and Your Adolescent,* p. 242.

6

Twenty Ways to Survive the Teenage Years

Do you remember the old joke about the boy who wrote his dad a letter from college: "Dear Dad, No mon. No fun. Your son."

In reply, his father wrote: "Dear Son, Too bad. So sad. Your Dad."

Well, I suppose just about every parent of a child who is away from home, whether he's at college, prep school, or at a two-week summer camp, has received a letter that says, basically, "Dear Mom and Dad. Please send money. Love . . . Junior."

It's interesting, isn't it. Adolescents want their parents to keep their distance, to stay out of their lives and let them make their own decisions. But just wait until they need something, and that's when they will come running to good old Mom and Dad.

And more often than not, good old Mom and Dad are ready and willing to meet the need.

One of the requirements for the job of being the parent of an adolescent is a thick skin. You cannot have your feelings hurt easily. You've got to remember that even when and if they don't act like it, your teenagers do need you, and for more reasons than that you're the one with all the money!

Adolescents sometimes seem to live on emotions. One day they're sky-high and the next they're valley-low. Consequently, the emotional life of the teenager is usually topsy-turvy, not by design but by their very nature, and often they end up hurting those who are closest to them, and that means Mom and Dad.

What's the best way for parents to handle these kids during their teenage years? The easiest way is to say, "If we just love them enough everything will work out okay." This could not be further from the truth. Love is not complete without discipline.

Now *discipline* doesn't mean to punish. It means to teach, to show the way, to disciple. Parents need to give guidelines, set limits, establish rules, and enforce them.

Guidelines are important because they communicate to our children that we care what happens to them. They may not always agree with the guidelines, but that's all right. They also need something to bounce off of, to resist if you will, because resistance is what builds strength. Regulations which teenagers resist will help keep them on a course that is instructive, not destructive, and will help them build the muscle they will need when they are out on their own, making their own decisions. So children, for their own sakes, must be taught to respect and obey parental authority.

There is a three-part message that we have to impart to our children: (1) They have to respect and obey us as their parents, (2) they are special people and, therefore, (3) they have a right to expect the best life has to offer them.

How do we parents go about setting up the guidelines that will impart these truths? The following are 20 tried-and-true steps you can take on a day-to-day basis with your children to get that message across.

1. Don't Threaten

If you say something is going to happen in the way of discipline, be sure that it happens. Don't say anything unless you intend to follow through. There's nothing worse than telling a child or adolescent that if he does something he's going to receive a certain punishment, seeing him go ahead and engage in the improper behavior, and then not doing anything about it. This teaches your child that your word doesn't really mean a thing, and it tells him that he doesn't have to pay any attention to those who are in authority. For your child's sake, think before you threaten. If major decisions need to be made, sleep on them for a night or two and discuss them with your spouse before the two of you approach your teenager to discuss the matter.

2. Watch Your Expectations

Many times parents unknowingly place unrealistic expectations on their children. Standards need to be realistic. You can't impose super-high expectations for your children and maintain an encouraging situation. We live in a world that is perfection-oriented, and most of us are great when it comes to picking out the flaws in others. Too many parents see nothing but the shortcomings of their teenagers and, by imposing unrealistic expectations on them, push them in the direction of personal disaster.

3. Accept Them Where They Are

It's tough to accept your child where he is. Strange, really, because we don't always have trouble accepting other people's children where they are . . . but we want ours to be different and better. Now I'm not saying, though, that you have to *agree* with the way your children are, but that you do have to communicate that you care for them. You may not love what your child is doing, but you still love your child, and when you communicate that message, you're letting him know that you accept him where he is. How many inconsequential battles have been fought over the way a teenager wanted to wear his hair? Far too many.

If your child or teenager has feelings or opinions which happen to collide with your own feelings or opinions, try to recognize that he has a right to feel and think for himself. Hear him out, accept him as he is, and then go on from there. If he is immature in the way he thinks, your understanding him and accepting him anyhow will go a long way toward helping him sort out his feelings. However, he may never totally agree with you.

4. Take Time to Listen

This ties in with accepting your child. If you want a relationship with your child—if you want to still be friends with him when he is grown, take the time to listen to him now. Listening means that your entire energy is geared toward just trying to hear and feel what he is trying to tell you. Don't be judgmental because you disagree, and don't spend your listening time preparing what you're going to say when he's finished talking. *Really* listen.

5. Respect Their Choices

This is tougher than it sounds. After all, we know what's best for our children. We've had to learn from our experience, and we'd rather spare them the pain of doing the same thing. If only they would listen to us . . . then maybe they wouldn't make such dumb choices. Right?

We know what clothes look best on our teenagers, we know what friends are best for our teenagers, we know what activities they should be taking part in. . . . When it gets right down to it, we know pretty much everything our children should do, say, and be. So why can't they just submit to us and let us live their lives for them?

There were some interesting studies done with elementary-school children who were told they could have anything they wanted for lunch from the school cafeteria. For one month, they didn't have to take anything but desserts if that's all they wanted. And for the first few days of the experiment, that's exactly what most of them did. But as the days went by, the kids began to swing back to a very traditional and well-balanced diet. You see, kids love to test us. They are going to selectively like things they know we don't like just to see if we will love them even though we disagree with them. They want us to respect their choices. Much rebellion during the teen years comes about because kids want their choices—right or wrong—to be respected. Your child can make dozens of "wrong" choices and still turn out to be a respectable adult you'll be proud to acknowledge as your son or daughter. I've seen it happen many times.

6. Ask for Forgiveness

Well, they aren't getting any easier, are they? Have you ever done anything wrong, parenting-wise? Have you ever blamed your child for something you found out later he didn't do? Have you ever been too busy to listen to him when he needed somebody to talk to? Have you ever "flown off the handle" and made a monstrous mountain out of a minute molehill? If you're human, of course you have. Well, don't you think your child deserves an apology when you do something like that?

145

The attitude of "I can say whatever I want to say because I'm your mother (or father)" just won't cut it.

I've seen what happens when a parent goes in a humble manner to a child and says, "Forgive me." It works wonders in the relationship. For us as parents to admit that we were insensitive, cruel, mean, forgetful—whatever—to our teenagers really makes us stand tall in their eyes. When we can openly admit that we blew it, all kinds of avenues open up for our children to share with us.

7. Respect Their Privacy

During the adolescent years, as emotions run high and new sexual feelings run rampant in an adolescent's body, your kids need you to step back and let them have their privacy. It's hard to handle the fact that your little boy or girl doesn't want to crawl into your lap anymore, or go for a ride in the family car, or do much of anything else with the family. You really get the feeling that the kid is only interested in having a place to sleep and eat—and maybe a message center, a place that will collect all his telephone messages for him. Well, that's perfectly normal. Your teenager is building his own independence while, at the same time, he's still under the shelter of your love and concern. Help him by respecting his privacy.

Unless you have reason to suspect that there is a major problem, do not read the notes from her friends that she leaves lying around in her room. Don't go through his drawers. Don't listen in on telephone conversations.

A mother told me she was very upset because she was going through her 14-year-old's drawers and found a couple of *Playboy* magazines. I'm no fan of that magazine, but as far as this boy was concerned, I told his mom that a couple of copies of a sexy magazine was no big deal. In fact, it was a sign of normal curiosity and sexual awareness. (If she had found whips and chains, well, that would have been another story.) I was more concerned over the mother's invasion of her son's privacy.

Give your teenagers room to grow. If you have always had a good relationship, and you have given them moral training, then chances are that they will not dive off into the deep end.

8. Share Your Feelings

If your teenager asks you how you feel about something, go ahead and tell him. If your daughter says, "How do I look?" and you think her skirt is way too short, don't lie and say she looks great. There's a world of difference between making up your child's opinion for him and in expressing your own feelings.

That reminds me of the story of a country church that struggled for over a year to buy a new chandelier for the sanctuary. They had a promotional campaign and already had the approval of the committee in charge of church expenditures. But it had to go before the congregation, and for an item as costly as this, 100 percent approval was required. The chairman of the church stood up and asked for the final vote. It was almost unanimous, but one old farmer in the back row voted no.

After a bit more discussion, the chairman called for another vote, and again the farmer voted no. Finally the chairman asked the old man as to why he was resisting buying the chandelier. The old fellow replied, "There's too many other things this church needs, like a light in the sanctuary."

What's my point? Speak directly to your kids. Call it as you see it. Don't try to dazzle them.

147

9. Do the Unexpected

Doing the unexpected can be a very good way of communicating respect to children and teenagers and also of making them accountable for the choices they make. For example, suppose Mom and Dad have asked their teenagers to get dinner started, but they come home from work and find the kids haven't done a thing. What should they do? I think they should say, "See you, kids. We're going out for dinner." And leave the kids there to fend for themselves. Chances are they'll find something in the refrigerator to fix themselves, and if they don't, missing one meal won't kill them. They'll certainly learn a lesson.

Doing the unexpected is a good way to grab their attention, to make a child think, "Wow! I guess they mean business about this!" It puts an end to the adolescent's attitude of "Yeah, yeah . . . I've heard it all before. So what else is new?" The unexpected is occasionally needed as a means of waking everyone up.

10. Talk About Potential Problems

As we've discussed before, it is important to talk to your children about some of the pitfalls and challenges that lie "just down the road." For instance, talking to a 13- or 14-year-old about some of the things that are likely to happen when he begins dating at 16 is a good thing to do. Such communication gives your child time to prepare and he'll be better able to make rational decisions when the time comes. Also, the teenager will be more receptive when you talk about problems before he has to meet them.

Again, here is an opportunity to share with them from your own life—something that is always beneficial. Tell them about some of the problems you faced and choices you made—good choices and bad.

11. Don't Act Like a Teenager

It's a temptation for many of us to feel that by not acting our age, we identify with our youngsters and make them feel comfortable with us. Actually the reverse is true. Kids who have parents that try to act, look, and talk like teenagers tell me that they feel very self-conscious and embarrassed when their moms or dads attempt to be cool. Most adolescents want their parents to act, look, and talk like parents. That's our role. They have plenty of buddies. They need parents.

12. Give Them Choices; Let Them Fail

Think about the time in your life when things began to come together for you. Was that time prompted by success or failure? If you're like most of us, the good and dramatic changes in your life came out of failure, as a result of what you learned from falling short.

For example, giving a teenager the choice of mowing the lawn or else paying someone else to mow it for him—out of his allowance—is a good technique. It says, "Hey, you have a choice. Do you want the privilege of paying someone else to do it for you, or do you want to do it yourself?" If I'm a teenager who spends all my allowance the first day on a new video game or compact disc, what's going to happen later in the week when all my friends want to go to the movies? I won't be able to go because I already spent all my money. I'm learning through the choices I make—good and bad— and when those choices are bad ones I've got to take the consequences.

There are real responsibilities and choices to be made out there in the world, and kids have to learn how to handle them while they're still in the home. It's the safest place in the world to learn about the realities of life.

13. Don't Snowplow Their School Road

When you get involved in a kid's schoolwork and activities, 90 percent of the time that involvement is negative involvement. It's important that children learn, early in their lives, that their schoolwork is their own responsibility, and no one else's.

I have never even asked my kids about their homework. That is their responsibility. If they need help with something they can ask for it, and they know that Sande and I are available.

I'm not saying that parents shouldn't see to it that a child sets aside time every day to do his homework, but parents should resist the temptation to help him with it or do it for him. Certain guidelines should be established. For instance, your child works on homework every evening between 7 and 8 P.M. and longer if necessary. But once that time has been established, it's the teenager's responsibility to adhere to his schedule. Homework should not be allowed to become a nightly battle.

Parents also ought to see to it that the schools encourage responsibility in their children. Not too long ago, I worked with some parents who literally had to beat on the high school principal's desk to get him to flunk their freshman son. All the boy's grades for the entire year were D's and F's. The kid wasn't learning according to the school's own report system, but school authorities were still going to promote him to a higher grade. Now, how are we ever going to teach accountability and responsibility training to our children when the school system tells them that no matter how badly they may do in class, they'll still be promoted to a higher grade? That's crazy!

14. Don't Show Them Off or Embarrass Them

It's easy to fall into the trap of showing off your children. I know that you're proud of their accomplishments, whatever they may be . . . but to ask your talented son or daughter to perform for your friends or relatives without first preparing them is putting them on the spot. You wouldn't like someone to put you on the spot that way. Why would you do it to your teenager?

The other side of this coin is not to embarrass them in front of others. For instance, Mom comes home from work and her 13-year-old son is out in the yard playing touch football with a group of his friends. She walks in the house and sees immediately that he's left a mess in the kitchen. She stalks back outside and lets him have it, right in front of his friends. Holding a dirty glass she starts in, "How many times have I told you, young man, that when you make a mess in the kitchen, you're supposed to clean it up. I work hard all day, and I don't want to have to come home and clean up your messes!" And on and on.

Is that effective? No way. Mom's anger is understandable, but she would be much wiser to wait until later to tell her son how she felt when she found the mess in the kitchen. How would you feel if you made a mistake at work, and your boss came out and browbeat you about it in front of your coworkers? Obviously, not very good. So don't do that sort of thing to your adolescent. Have the courtesy to wait until you're alone with him and then, if he needs chewing out, go ahead. A good chewing out never hurts. Tell him exactly how you feel about things.

15. Don't Be a Flaw-picker

Chances are that your teen has a pretty good idea of his own flaws. In fact, chances are good that he sees them through a high-powered magnifying glass. He doesn't need his mother and father pouncing on every little thing he does. Remember that adolescence is generally a time of very low self-esteem.

Children and adolescents need to be reminded, coaxed, and encouraged to do what they should. They don't need to have someone constantly point out their weaknesses, failures, and flaws.

16. Don't Spit in Their Soup

What do I mean by this?

"Mom, can I go to the dance?"

"Sure, honey . . . you go and have a good time. But please be careful because you know how I worry about you when you're out at night."

Is that girl going to have a good time at the dance? Probably not. She'll be too busy feeling guilty about "poor old Mom," who's pacing the floor at home, worrying about her. Spitting in the soup is a sure way to create the guilties in your children and put up boundaries between you and your kids.

Another thing we as parents do is to dig up old bones.

"Well, I suppose you can go to the dance . . . but last time you were three minutes late getting home!" That sort of thing. There's no need to be dredging up the past at every opportunity. Think about what you're doing, parents, before you spit in your child's soup or dig up some old bones.

17. Don't Talk in Volumes

Parents have a good way of overdoing things. If your adolescent asks what time it is, tell him what time it is. Don't start quoting the theory of relativity from the latest book by Stephen Hocking, or tell him how Big Ben was made and how it's maintained. Many of us just wait for an opening as innocent as "What time is it?" to bring down volumes of advice and instructions. If you talk in volumes, your adolescent will tune you out immediately. And even though it's good to share with your child from your own experiences, try not to start out with the infamous words, "When I was your age . . ." Those five words are an immediate turnoff.

18. Share Your Real Self

When you're brave enough to share with your adolescent your real thoughts and feelings about yourself, you'll pave the way for honest, open communication between you. I know this is a difficult thing to do, because we would rather keep our skeletons hidden away in the closet, where they belong. But I believe that much in the way of comfort and encouragement can be given to a child or adolescent when he sees that his parents are human, and that they, too, make mistakes.

19. Don't Praise Your Adolescent

I realize that most of us grew up feeling that praise was important. In fact, I've seen bumper stickers that say, "Look for the good and praise it." It sounds great, but I've discovered that praise can be a very defeating thing for your adolescent. How do you feel when someone praises you? I feel very uneasy—that there's a hitch in it somewhere.

Encouragement is a good substitute for praise, and the difference is subtle. For instance, suppose you come home and find that your 13-year-old surprised you by cleaning up the kitchen, and she did a great job. You're overwhelmed, and so you say, "Honey, I can't believe it. I love you for this, Mary Louise. Here's five dollars for the great job you did."

Can you guess what's going to happen? The very next

night when Mom comes home Mary Louise is going to say, "Hey, Mom, where's my five dollars?"

"What five dollars?"

"The five dollars for today."

"What?"

"Well, yesterday you gave me five dollars for cleaning up, and I've done it again today. So where's my five dollars?"

That's the sort of problem you've created if you've gone into a relationship with your adolescent that is based on praise.

Now, let's go back to the day of the first kitchen-cleaning.

Mom calls her daughter to her and says, "It's such a joy to come home and see a clean, sparkling kitchen. I just want you to know that I appreciate your effort." And she gives her daughter a hug.

What does that communicate? It says that Mom noticed what her daughter did and she appreciates it. But notice that the emphasis is on her *effort* and not on the *job* she did.

The danger in praising an adolescent is that he might see himself as being loved or appreciated simply because he did the dishes, and that isn't true. We love our adolescents regardless of whether or not they do extra work. Encouragement is far better than praise.

20. Don't Make Mountains Out of Molehills

Some parents act like it's World War III when their adolescent does one thing wrong. I always tell parents of smaller children that when a kid knocks over a glass of milk at the table, he needs a rag so he can clean it up. He doesn't need an angry lecture from his parents.

The same advice applies to adolescents.

What do you say when your son hands you his report card and he has three *A*'s and one *C*? Do you get red in the face,

154

grab your chest, and scream, "Oh, no! A *C*! What's with this *C*?" It would be better to say, "Three *A*'s and a *C*! I'm really glad to see that you enjoy learning. I'll bet you're proud of your effort."

Chances are that your teenager will fall right over on the floor out of sheer amazement. Think about that for a second. Three superior efforts and only one average effort. That's really a good report card. But many of us would feel compelled to go to the *C* and respond to it rather than to the three *A*'s. Look to the good when you can, and avoid making a molehill or a "federal case" out of something that is relatively insignificant.

HANDLING THOSE INEVITABLE HASSLES

With an adolescent in the home there are going to be conflicts. That's just the way it is. But when a hassle develops and you're feeling that uneasiness between yourself and your child, try to approach the situation with a positive attitude. Pick a time and a place to discuss the problem where both of you are comfortable and can do so without interruption.

First, give your teenager the opportunity to tell his side of things. Begin by saying, "Robert, I'm very interested in what your feelings were and the reasons for your throwing your younger brother in the creek." After your adolescent describes his feelings or reasons, take time to reflect back on what you hear. Give him a chance to clarify so that you understand exactly what he's trying to say.

Next, ask him to listen to your point of view. Again, remember that while you are listening to him you aren't thinking about what you're going to say—you're just concentrating on listening.

When you give your side, try to be as specific as you can about why you're bothered by the problem. Don't be general. If you're general, you're going to leave room for misinterpretation and inaccuracy. Take time to discuss how you would have liked to see the problem handled if you could turn the clock back—which you can't. Then give your adolescent the opportunity to tell how he should have handled the problem.

Lastly, work toward a mutual solution to the problem. That's why you and your teenager sat down and talked about the problem to begin with, so that you could come to an agreeable solution. There might have to be some compromise or some negotiation, but that's true of almost everything in life. If there is some doubt in your mind or your adolescent's mind as to what is expected, take the time to write out the agreement and sign it. Then if there's a need to go back later and refer to it, everyone knows exactly what was expected.

I hope these guidelines are useful to you as you go through the teen years with your adolescent. Being a teenager or being a parent of a teenager is not a very easy task and it requires a great amount of determination and willingness to cooperate, as well as much love and understanding, to survive those years!

TAKE ACTION

—Ask your adolescent to draw up a list for you of his "20 Rules for Parenting Teenagers." Ask him what he thinks you should and shouldn't do—what he likes and what he doesn't like about the way you relate to him. Then sit down and discuss his "rules" with him, finding out why he feels as he does about certain things, and pledging to modify your behavior where appropriate.

—After dinner some night, have each member of the family list on a piece of paper all the attributes and characteristics he or she wants others to think he or she has. Then, on the other side of the paper, have each list all the attributes and characteristics he *really* sees in himself. Then have parents and children exchange papers. This exercise should generate some interesting discussion. As you explain why you said what you said about yourself, take the opportunity to tell some funny, amusing, or even dumb stories about your childhood and adolescent years.

7

Drinking and Drugs = Danger and Death

Sometime back, I worked with a high school senior who had gone to a party on the University of Arizona campus.

This young woman wanted to "be cool," to fit in with everybody else, so she walked around all evening with a drink in her hand, sipping it. As many new drinkers do, she guzzled a bit too much too quickly and wound up passing out. Some "gentlemen," who were obviously concerned for her welfare, thought enough of her to take her to their apartment.

There they removed her clothing and, as best as we could determine, about 10 young men gang-raped this 17-year-old girl.

Several hours later when she woke up all she had were some faint and frightening memories of what had transpired. What an ugly blemish and memory this young girl has to face. Why? Because she acted irresponsibly. She went along with the crowd and didn't use her head.

Now I realize that if you were to tell your adolescent a story like that, you might get nothing more in reaction than a sarcastic laugh or a remark such as, "Oh, come on, Mom.

I'm not *stupid.* I wouldn't let anything like that happen to me."

Teenagers think these "horror" stories are things that we adults have made up, just to stop them from having fun.

But that's not true. The horror stories are real, and many of them are brought about by the use of drugs and alcohol. Anyone who doesn't believe it should look into this young girl's eyes and see the pain and anguish she feels.

And there are more horror stories being added every day.

For example, the leading cause of death among young people is drinking and driving. Drinking is so widespread that a national survey of high-school seniors found that more than 90 percent had tried alcohol; half said they drank every week; 37 percent said they had had five or more drinks on at least one occasion in the last two weeks; and 5 percent said that they drank every day. That survey also discovered that 10 to 25 percent of those between the ages of 11 and 13 had tried alcohol.[1]

Furthermore, it has been determined that roughly 60 percent of these same high school seniors have tried marijuana, and a substantial number have tried hallucinogens, uppers, downers, cocaine, and even heroin.[2]

Doctors Raymond B. Johnson and William Lukash, in a booklet, *Medical Complications of Alcohol Abuse,* say that "alcohol can be a catalyst for violence of all types. There are at least 100,000 alcohol-related deaths in the United States each year: 50 percent of the homicides in the United States are alcohol-related, and 50 percent of all the felons in federal penitentiaries have alcohol-related problems. One-third of the suicide victims in this country show significant alcohol intoxication."[3]

STARTING YOUNG

Claire Costales, author of *Staying Dry*, says that she became an alcoholic at 17 when she began sneaking drinks from parties her parents held in her home—or from parties in friends' homes which she attended with her family. She says that "if booze hadn't been presented to me as acceptable, helpful, and glamorous, chances are I would not have chosen a career in alcoholism."[4]

This tells me that the burden of informing—modeling as well as teaching—our children about this great threat to their happiness, their health, and their very lives is on us, their parents. Remember that children and adolescents copy what is modeled for them, and the earliest modeling they have is in the home. If very young children see one or both of their parents socializing over liquor, offering it to their guests, they will naturally assume that that's the proper way to act.

What happens in this situation is that the child can't wait to be "all grown up" so he can drink. In fact, he may come to see drinking, along with driving, as the two signs of adulthood, and that is a very dangerous mix. If he sees drinking as a grown-up behavior, he is not likely to turn it down the first time one of his friends offers him a beer or a swig from a bottle of vodka or whiskey.

Again, remember that it is important to talk to your children about the dangers of alcohol when they are very young. Then try to keep the avenues of communication open between you so that your adolescent can share with you some of the stories and incidents he becomes aware of at school. And pay attention to his lifestyle. You remember that in the last chapter I urged you to respect your child's pri-

160

vacy, but I also said that the privacy could be invaded if you felt that there was a major problem.

If you suspect that your child is drinking or using other drugs, you cannot think, "Well, that's his business." It's not. It's your business, and this is one time you have to break down that wall of privacy and be confrontational.

I'm not suggesting that you should "fly all to pieces" if you suspect that your adolescent has had one drink. It's not a time for emotionalism. Remember that more than 90 percent of kids at least try alcohol before their high school days are through, and one drink doesn't mean that your child is going to turn into a drunk. But sit down with the child, tell him what you suspect, and then as calmly and rationally as possible explain why you want him to stay as far away from drinking as possible.

A few reasons:

- It's illegal for you to drink.
- Drinking is not good for your health.
- Driving when you've been drinking or being a passenger in the car with someone who's been drinking can get you seriously injured or even killed.
- You are not in complete control of yourself when you've been drinking, and you might get into some sort of trouble. (Just as happened to the girl I told you about at the beginning of this chapter.)
- Alcohol can be addictive.

BE ALERT

Professionals who work with teenage problem drinkers suggest a number of areas where parents should be alert.

161

Among them are: know if your teenagers are attending school each day; see if they are defensive when questioned about alcohol; be aware of behavioral changes, such as extreme boredom, moodiness, or exhaustion; know where they are going and with whom; be present if there is a party at your house; if they ever get into a situation where they have had too much to drink and they call you to come pick them up, do so without recriminations.

If you should happen to find your teenager drunk, take care of his immediate needs and then get him to bed. The next day, while his head is still pounding from the night before, be direct and straightforward with him about what happened.

Now as I've been talking about teenage drinkers, I've been using the generic "he." But alcohol abuse is a growing problem among women. Between 1975 and 1985, the number of college females who could be described as "hard drinking" tripled,[5] and there is no reason to suspect that it has lessened since then. And if that's what's going on among college-age women, it's fairly safe to assume that the same thing is going on with high-school girls.

According to Dr. Eleanor Hanna, Director of the Alcohol Clinic of Massachusetts General Hospital, "There is a total naïveté among many female patients who come to our clinic about their physiological inability to tolerate as much alcohol as a man."[6]

Dr. Hanna points out that there are significant differences between men and women when it comes to the ability to tolerate alcohol. For one thing, men are apparently able to maintain a constant level of alcohol tolerance, whereas the level women can tolerate varies greatly. This can be due partly to the menstrual cycle, and partly to the use of oral contraceptives. Therefore, drinking alcohol is a greater

162

threat to the female than it is to the male—and it *is* a threat
to the male!

HOW CAN YOU KNOW?

How can your teenager know if alcohol is a problem for
him? More importantly, how can *you* know?

Alcoholics Anonymous distributes a sheet prepared by
Johns Hopkins University—a self-test to determine if someone is a problem drinker. Of course, for the following test to
do any good, the questions must be answered as honestly as
possible:

1. Do you lose time from work (or school) due to drinking?

2. Is drinking making your home life unhappy?

3. Do you drink because you are shy with other people?

4. Is drinking affecting your reputation?

5. Have you ever felt remorse after drinking?

6. Have you gotten into financial difficulties as a result
of drinking?

7. Do you turn to lower companions and an inferior environment when drinking?

8. Does your drinking make you careless of your family's welfare?

9. Has your ambition decreased since drinking?

10. Do you crave a drink at a definite time daily?

11. Do you want a drink the next morning?

12. Does drinking cause you to have difficulty in sleeping?

13. Has your efficiency decreased since drinking?

14. Is drinking jeopardizing your job or business (or schoolwork)?

15. Do you drink to escape from worries or troubles?

16. Do you drink alone?

17. Have you ever had a complete loss of memory as a result of drinking?

18. Has your doctor ever treated you for drinking?

19. Do you drink to build up your self-confidence?

20. Have you ever been to a hospital or institution on account of drinking?

A yes to any one of these questions is a definite warning that the person taking the test may be an alcoholic. Two yes answers indicate that the test-taker probably is an alcoholic. If the person taking the test answered yes to three or more questions and wants to stop drinking, he or she should call the local office of AA or write to Alcoholics Anonymous, P.O. Box 459, Grand Central Station, New York, NY 10017.

OTHER DRUG PROBLEMS

Alcohol is the most abused drug in the United States and is the drug of choice among American teenagers, followed very closely by tobacco, with marijuana third on the list and cocaine fourth.

You remember Chuck, whose transcript I shared with you back in Chapter Four. Let's go back to Chuck now, for more of his story:

"I started getting high on drugs when I was a freshman in high school. I guess if you were to ask me why I started getting high I'd say it was probably because everybody else was doing it, it was the thing to do, and you weren't cool if you weren't doing it. Before I let peer pressure take over I used to enjoy telling people that I didn't get high or drink and didn't smoke cigarettes. I can still say truthfully that I've never smoked a whole cigarette—and don't guess I've taken five hits off a cigarette in my whole life. But with dope you weren't cool if you didn't participate.

"I have to admit the first couple of times I tried pot I didn't get too much out of it, but I kept on doing it and kept on doing it until it got to be where it was a fun thing to do. I'd go to parties and at first I'd really laugh a lot and it was just a good time. My friends and I would get giggly and all that stuff. The first couple of months it was a lot of fun—it was a cool thing to do. Instead of going to class we'd go out and catch a 'buzz.' When we came back everybody saw we had red eyes and thought we were cool. So it was really neat to walk into class and let everybody know we were high. You know how everybody does, they walk up to you and talk so they blow their breath on you to let you know they were out getting high at lunch. . . .

"It wasn't until a couple of years later that I really started having bad feelings about marijuana—I wasn't smart enough to see what it was doing to me but I could sure see what it was doing to my friends. It seemed that a lot of procrastination was happening in their lives. We'd get high in the morning and just kind of waste the day, just breeze through the whole day, not really accomplishing anything, just lie there and watch TV, go play ball, or do nothing. And you can't really live today tomorrow. I really feel strongly that you should accomplish something, whether it's learning something, bettering yourself physically or mentally or whatever. Inside I didn't feel good about just sitting around all day and not doing anything. And that was pretty common with marijuana."

Chuck found out what many scientists and physicians

165

have now proven—that marijuana creates a particular personality in its users. In some people, the effects do not show up for several years; in others the personality impairment is almost immediate. These distinct traits are called "pot personality" symptoms, and they include impaired short-term memory, emotional flatness, the drop-out syndrome—out of sports, out of school, out of family—diminished willpower, concentration, attention span, ability to deal with abstract or complex problems, increased confusion in thinking, impaired judgment, and hostility toward authority.[7]

And then, of course, there is cocaine, and specifically crack—the drug that killed basketball superstar Len Bias a few years ago.

Crack is rapidly becoming the drug of choice among some teenagers, especially those who live in urban areas. It's a particularly potent form of cocaine, and teens who have smoked it tell me that they felt extreme power and intense exhilaration after doing so. The problem is that crack is highly addictive, and can lead to side effects such as depression, psychosis, heart failure, respiratory collapse—and death.

Cocaine is, of course, *the* drug most often used by upper-middle-class Americans—and at what price? Not only are users of cocaine damaging their own health, but the battle for control of the drug market results in hundreds (perhaps thousands) of deaths every year. Most of us have been aghast over the last years and months as we've read about the violence and destruction that has resulted from Colombia's war against its own cocaine cartels.

Some of the old drugs from the 60s are still around too. LSD has made somewhat of a comeback on high school and college campuses, along with other hallucinogenic drugs.

And then there are:

- Barbiturates, otherwise known as "downers." These include such brand name drugs as Doridan, Nembutal, and Seconal, and are highly addictive. They bring on a state of euphoria and relaxation, accompanied by impaired coordination and slurred speech.
- Narcotics, including Demerol, heroin, methadone, morphine, opium, and Percodan. These, too, are highly addictive, and may cause euphoria, hallucinations, and decreased alertness.
- Amphetamines or "uppers," such as Benzedrine, Dexedrine, and Preludin. These drugs are sometimes referred to as "speed" because they give the user a sense of excitement and nervous energy. Teens who are on amphetamines may exhibit rapid speech, insomnia, decreased appetite, and even convulsions. These, too, are highly addictive, and long-term use can result in severe psychosis.
- Antidepressants include Elavil, Ritalin, and Tofranil, and although they are not addictive, prolonged use may cause damage to the heart and liver, as well as hinder the body's ability to manufacture white blood cells.
- Inhalants, including airplane glue and other aerosols. One of the more recent ways for kids to get high is by sniffing freon from heat pumps. Inhalants can cause liver, kidney, bone marrow, and brain damage, and although they are not physically addictive, there is a very high chance that a person who uses an inhalant will become psychologically addicted.

In their book *You and Your Adolescent,* Dr. Laurence Steinberg and Ann Levine give a list of danger signs for concerned parents who want to be able to spot the signs of drug abuse. That list is well worth repeating here:[8]

DRUGS AND DRUG PARAPHERNALIA

• Possession of pipes, rolling papers, small decongestant bottles, small butane torches, or other drug-related items
• Possession or evidence of drugs, such as butts, seeds, or leaves in ashtrays or clothing pockets, or unidentified pills or powders in plastic bags
• Odor of drugs or use of cover-ups (incense, sprays)

Identification with Drug Culture

• Possession of drug-related magazines, slogans, slogans on clothing
• Preoccupation with drugs in conversations and jokes
• Hostility in discussing drugs

Signs of Physical Deterioration

• Memory lapses, short attention span, difficulty concentrating
• Poor physical coordination, slurred and incoherent speech (incomplete sentences, forgotten thoughts, bizarre statements)
• Unhealthy appearance; changes in appetite and weight
• Bloodshot eyes, dilated pupils, runny nose, hacking cough, increased susceptibility to colds and infections
• Changes in activity levels (periods of lethargy and fatigue and/or periods of hyperactivity)

Dramatic Changes in School Performance

• Distinct downward turn in grades, not just from *C*'s
to *F*'s, but also from *A*'s and *B*'s to *C*'s; assignments not
completed
• Increased absenteeism or tardiness

Changes in Behavior

• Chronic dishonesty (lying, stealing, cheating; trouble
with police)
• Changes in friends, evasiveness in talking about new
ones
• Possession of large amounts of money
• Increasing and inappropriate anger, hostility, irrita-
bility, secretiveness
• Mood swings—from overly happy and gregarious to
morose and withdrawn
• Reduced motivation, self-discipline, self-esteem
• Indifference to hygiene and grooming
• Loss of interest in favorite extracurricular activities
and hobbies

WHAT CAN PARENTS DO?

Studies I have read indicate that the closer the adolescent
is to his or her parents, the less likely it is that he or she will
use drugs. That really says something, doesn't it?

If you're not taking the time to talk to your children about
drugs you'd better start. Drugs are as accessible to children
and adolescents today as Hershey bars were available to my
generation. Talk to your kids about drugs, about the values

you want them to have, and show them the articles in the newspapers about people dying because of alcohol and drug abuse. I've already mentioned Len Bias, but there are many other examples, including Jim Morrison, whose life and death was brought back to the public's attention via Oliver Stone's recent movie, *The Doors.*

Several years ago, it was my unfortunate task to call a mother and father in the Midwest and notify them that their son had overdosed. You see, he didn't pay much attention to what many professionals have tried to explain, that the combination of booze and drugs is a deadly one. This young man had several beers and then popped some barbiturates. Early in the morning his roommate returned from his night on the town and noticed something very peculiar about this young man—his neck was blue. He was dead. A 19-year-old's life was snuffed out because he was irresponsible. I'd be willing to bet that his parents never took the time to talk with their son about the deadly nature of drugs.

Perhaps those parents didn't know where to begin or didn't have the necessary information. There's no excuse for that today, because every community has much in the way of information regarding drug use. Ask your family doctor or the local community health service—or check your local library. You ought to find plenty of materials which can serve as a springboard to further discussion with your adolescents.

How do you begin to talk to your adolescent about drugs? First, let him know that you really care about him as a person and would like to know how he feels about drug use. If teenagers see that their parents want to be close to them and really do love them, chances are that they will open up, share their thoughts, and be responsive to what their parents want to teach them. These are the kids who are more than likely not going to get involved with drugs.

If you suspect that your child has a problem with drugs and alcohol, I suggest you get professional help as soon as possible. In the meantime, there are some other steps you should take:

• Suspend driving privileges until your son or daughter has demonstrated a willingness to stay drug-free and sober.

• Make sure you know where he or she is every minute of the day. If he tells you he's going to "Fred's house," give him time to get there, and then call Fred's house to see if he's there. Make sure that he checks in with you at prearranged frequencies—say every 60 or 90 minutes. This will allow you the opportunity to see if he exhibits slurred speech or a tendency to ramble. If he does, ask where he is and tell him that you are going to come pick him up.

• Monitor the way he or she spends money. If you suspect that allowance money is going for drugs, then cut back on the allowance or dispense with it altogether.

• Set specific penalties that will be imposed for violating your no-drugs policy, and then stick to them.

HELP THEM MAKE THE RIGHT CHOICE

The reality of life today is that drugs are easily available — and that means your kids are going to have to make a choice as to whether or not they will use them. They are going to have to have the courage of their convictions to say, "No, I don't want to be like everyone else and just follow along." But they need your help.

Most of us have heard the story of Carol Burnett's life, how both her parents were alcoholics and the only stabilizing factor in her life was her grandmother.

Carrie, Carol's own daughter, started using drugs at age 13. By the time she had reached 14 she had an intense drug problem for which she was hospitalized. In an interview, Carol was asked if she blamed herself for her daughter's problem with drugs. She answered, "I did at first." Then she said she realized that her daughter was trying to cop out with the excuse that she took drugs because her mother was famous, and she, too, was thrust into the limelight and couldn't handle it.

Carol said, "Tell me, who lives a normal life? I never did! I would rather my parents had been me and I had lived the kind of life my kids have than to have grown up as I did. Everybody is born with something they have to overcome." Then she said something that I think is very significant: "It's their [the kids'] responsibility [to take charge of their own lives]. I had to deal with my parents—I don't blame them. I did what I could with myself. All kids have to do the same. . . . Everybody finds something to complain about—that's human nature. But we are all responsible for ourselves."[9]

How true! We are all responsible for ourselves. But parents are responsible for teaching their kids to be responsible— and if you've not been doing a good job of that, resolve that you're going to turn things around—and do it today!

TAKE ACTION

• If you've never taken time to talk to your children about alcohol and drugs, now would be a good time to start. If you don't know where to begin, plan today to take your children, one at a time, away somewhere overnight or for a weekend, for a combination of fun and serious talk. While you're in the car driving to your weekend spot, when you can't look at each other eyeball-to-eyeball, begin to open up. Talk turkey about the subjects you've been avoiding. There is something magical about frank discussions with others while you're out driving.

• Make a trip to your local library to see what information they have on drug abuse. Call a family meeting and share this information with your children. Encourage your kids to talk openly about the pressures they may feel from others to drink or take drugs, and answer their questions as to why they should abstain from drugs.

• If you smoke or drink, quit. It may not be easy, but it will be very much worth the effort, both for your sake and for the sake of your children.

1. Laurence Steinberg and Ann Levine, *You and Your Adolescent,* p. 119.
2. Douglas H. Powell, *Teenagers: When to Worry and What to Do,* p. 223.
3. Raymond B. Johnson and William Lukash, *Medical Complications of Alcohol Abuse, summary of 1973 AMA Washington Conference,* p. 6.
4. Claire Costales, *Staying Dry* (Ventura, Calif.: Regal Books, 1980), p. 30.
5. Douglas H. Powell, p. 223.
6. Eleanor Hanna, *Massachusetts General Hospital News,* September 1981.
7. Peggy Mann, "Marijuana Alert III: The Devastation of Personality," *Reader's Digest* (December 1981), p. 81.
8. Steinberg and Levine, p. 271.
9. Dotson Rader, "The Triumph of Carol Burnett," *Parade* (January 5, 1982), p. 7.

8

You Are Something Special

This is an open letter to your adolescents. Encourage them to read it. Better yet, read and discuss it with them.

Take a look around you. Don't you feel like most people are happier than you are? As I said to your parents earlier in this book, adolescence is a time when things are exaggerated—when other people really do seem better off than you. That feeling is only natural due to the great amount of insecurity and uncertainty in an adolescent's life. But it's not always going to be this way.

Think about Mom and Dad for a moment. It's hard to believe that at one time in their lives they also felt ugly, unwanted, rejected, and insecure. Now if they have followed the suggestions I've given in this book, they have already shared with you the real self-images and thoughts they had about themselves when they were growing up.

CHANGING RELATIONSHIPS AND VALUES

Of course, what's of prime importance to most teenagers are those very special relationships they form during high school days—not only with friends of the opposite sex, but friends of the same sex as well. Once your high school days are ended, however, as hard as it may be for you to believe it now, those relationships will pretty much come to an end. There will be a fracturing of the friends whom you now think will be your lifetime buddies. All of a sudden they'll vanish as they leave your community and go away to school, take jobs in various parts of the country, or get married. The whole gang will just sort of vanish into thin air. You'll be lucky to see some of them at 10-year intervals at the old high school reunion.

Speaking of that 10-year high school reunion, it may seem like a million years away, but you really have a choice to make right now. How do you want to be seen at that high school reunion, when you walk in there with your husband or wife? Do you want to meet previous lovers eyeball-to-eyeball? Or do you want to walk into a room where there are many people with whom you've had good times, without any skeletons in your closet? You don't have to look into anybody's eyes who will make you feel guilty or angry or hurt or any of those things—at least not as a direct result of sexual activity with them.

Your big advantage right now as a teenager is to realize that your virginity is yours, and there's nothing wrong with wanting to save yourself for marriage. The fact remains that once you fork it over, you can't get it back. You really have to decide right now whether you want sex to be really special and sacred, something to look forward to, or if you want it to become something dirty and nasty—a guilt-ridden experience.

I think you probably realize that the years ahead are going to mean many changes for you. Right now you might judge a restaurant by whether or not it has video machines in the lobby. But 10 years from now you may be more impressed by the bearnaise sauce. All of us, whether we like to admit it or not, are going to do a lot of changing between graduation and the first high school reunion. Take pride in the fact that you are special and different and not like anybody else.

MUCH TO LOOK FORWARD TO

So as you approach adulthood and freedom and independence, I hope you do it with optimism and with a great deal of excitement, because there is an awful lot in life to enjoy and benefit from.

Of course, many new experiences are exciting, but there are some scary ones too. The good news is that at the end of this long tunnel called adolescence there is a world that can be what you want it to be—a world where you can be happy and have self-worth and an opportunity to accomplish some of the things you'd like to in life. Adolescence isn't forever, thank goodness! Things have to get better, don't they? Can you believe there will be a time in your life when pimples will become a thing of the past? That's reason enough to celebrate, isn't it?

BIRDS OF A FEATHER

Someone once said that "birds of a feather flock to-gether," and it's true. If you really are concerned about having a good reputation, then be selective about your friends and associates. I realize there is a tremendous amount of pressure to be like everybody else. You know, 30 years ago, if somebody smoked pot or engaged in casual sex, people were really surprised. Surprised? Actually it would be more like it to say they were shocked and offended.

The tragic thing today is that it's become reversed. If you don't go along with the group and smoke dope and be like everybody else, people have a hard time believing that you don't. But you don't need to go along with your friends when you know that the things they are doing, the choices they are making, will only cause you harm.

BUILDING STRENGTH

There are going to be temptations, and you can't rely on Mom and Dad alone as you deal with these situations face-to-face, one-on-one. You're going to have to build your own strength and courage to say no to things you know aren't good for you. As you approach major decisions in your life, move slowly on them. Realize that it's normal right now for you to be impatient, to want to get everything done right away—but fight that tendency with conscious, rational thought. You can sleep on a decision before you make it. You can talk things over with your best friends or your parents. In some cases, your best friends might really be your parents. Maybe you have the kind of relationship where you can talk with them about anything. I certainly hope so.

WE NEED EACH OTHER

I also hope this book has helped both you and your parents to be able to talk on an honest level, taking off the many masks we all wear. As one 15-year-old girl said, "Boy, if my mom and dad knew what I did, they'd die." They probably wouldn't die. They'd probably understand. They've probably been through some of the same trials and tribulations you're going through right now.

A final note: Realize and accept the fact that, like everyone else, you are imperfect and need others in your life. I know you like to be cool and to act like you don't have a worry in the world. But those of us who work with teenagers on a daily basis know that there are plenty of worries in your life. You have to realize that if you try to shoulder all of those worries yourself, it's going to be a long, tough road. It might even be an impossible road. Share your thoughts and your burdens with your parents and seek direction in your life.

May the rocky road of your adolescent years be tolerable, and provide you with great learning experiences that will reinforce your understanding of real love.

You are something special—very special. Don't ever put yourself in a position where you are used by someone or where you are using someone. Always remember—people are for loving . . . not for using.

A TEENAGER'S TEN COMMANDMENTS TO PARENTS

1. Please don't give me everything I say I want. Saying no shows me you care. I appreciate guidelines.

2. Don't treat me like a little kid. Even though you know what's "right," I need to discover some things for myself.

3. Respect my need for privacy. I often need to be alone to sort things out and to daydream.

4. Never say, "In my day . . ." That's an immediate turnoff. Besides, the pressures and responsibilities of my world are more complicated.

5. I don't pick your friends or clothes, please don't criticize mine. We can disagree and still respect each other's choices.

6. Refrain from always rescuing me; I learn most from my mistakes. Hold me accountable for the decisions I make in life, it's the only way I'll learn to be responsible.

7. Be brave enough to share your disappointments, thoughts, and feelings with me. I'm never too old to be told I'm loved.

8. Don't talk in volumes. I've had years of good instruction, now trust me with the wisdom you have shared.

9. I respect you when you ask me for forgiveness for a thoughtless deed on your part. It proves that neither of us is perfect.

10. Set a good example. I pay more attention to your actions than your words.

For information regarding speaking engagements or seminars, write or call:

Dr. Kevin Leman
7355 N. Oracle #205
Tucson, AZ 85704
(602) 797-3830